Endorsements

"Families discover and embrace foster care adoption for many reasons. The common thread is the desire to give a child a home and to create a family. Mrs. Reeves' book not only examines, step by step, the process of adopting from the foster care system, but connects with everyone as she weaves her personal journey throughout. This will be a useful and comforting tool for any family thinking about adopting a foster care child."
Rita Soronen, Executive Director, Dave Thomas Foundation for Adoption

"Daphine Reeves offers a fresh and honest perspective on the process of adopting a child through a governmental agency. The same dedication and diligence with which she and Dirk approached PRIDE training is evident in the writing of this book. I highly recommend *Journeying Through State Adoption* as a resource to anyone considering state adoption!"
Jeanette M. Willis, Executive Director, National One Church One Child Texas

"This book is a useful tool for families who are beginning the journey of bringing a child into their lives through adoption. It allows parents to "get their feet wet" one toe at a time, and is written in a style that is encouraging and supportive of all types of families."
Jeanette Wiedemeier Bower, Project Manager, Adoption Subsidy Resource Center, North American Council on Adoptable Children (NACAC)

"It was an easy read, highly informative, and with just the right touch of personal perspectives to make it interesting and applicable."
Sylvia R. Franzmeier, Parent Group Manager, The Collaboration UsKids, Houston, Texas

Journeying Through
State Adoption

Journeying Through State Adoption

✦

Working With the System—One Day at a Time

Daphine L. Reeves

iUniverse, Inc.
New York Lincoln Shanghai

Journeying Through State Adoption
Working With the System—One Day at a Time

iUniverse books may be ordered through booksellers or by contacting:

iUniverse
2021 Pine Lake Road, Suite 100
Lincoln, NE 68512
www.iuniverse.com
1-800-Authors (1-800-288-4677)

ISBN-13: 978-0-595-37700-8 (pbk)
ISBN-13: 978-0-595-82083-2 (ebk)
ISBN-10: 0-595-37700-9 (pbk)
ISBN-10: 0-595-82083-2 (ebk)

Printed in the United States of America

To my wonderful husband, Dirk, who has always believed in me. Without your commitment to our family, I would not have been able to endure the challenges I faced in writing this book.

To my daughter, Morgan, who was my little cheerleader. Without your support, this book would still be no more than a dream.

And to my daughter, Jaelyn, who became part of our happy family. Without you, this journey would have never become a reality.

Contents

Acknowledgments

I would like to thank the following people for helping make this book possible:

Melanie Martin, my editor. Thank you for taking on this long and stressful task with me and for believing in this book from the very beginning. Thank you for always being patient and constantly re-editing when I kept changing things in every chapter.

Courteney Holden, for taking time out of your busy schedule to read my manuscript, for allowing me to use your expertise in the world of foster/adoption, and for believing in this book enough to contribute to it.

Janice Brown, Texas State Adoption Manager, for reviewing my manuscript. Thanks for your kind and honest support.

Jeanette Willis, for having faith in my family from day one in our PRIDE training. Thank you for the person you are and for what you give to so many other adoptive parents.

Deatra Gills, for being a constant listener to all that I had to say while writing this book.

Sylvia Franzmeier, for your honest input and many words of encouragement.

Rita Soronen, for your kind words of encouragement from the very beginning.

Jeanette Wiedemeier, for taking the time to read my manuscript and for offering your invaluable advice.

Josh Kroll, for leading me to Courteney Holden.

Michelle Gochis, Red Feather Photography, for doing such a wonderful job with the pictures for the front and back covers of this book.

Kristina Oberg, my illustrator. Thank you for accepting this task at the last minute and for doing such an awesome job in such a short time.

Ruby Webb, who was always eager to hear about what part of the book I was currently working on.

Angie Spinks, for being such a wonderful and dear friend and for being my head cheerleader in everything that I set out to accomplish.

To my mom, Froney Brown, for choosing to sacrifice and struggle in so many ways as a single parent. Without your determination and desire to make sure that

I had the necessities in life (mostly your love), what kind of person would I be today?

To all the adoptive parents for being committed to the kids who deserve a permanent and loving home.

I know that there are others that I have overlooked and I want to say "thank you" to each person who helped in any way, big or small.

God bless.

Foreword

It was not until I worked in the field of adoption that I became acutely aware that such a unique and beautiful experience could come from so much pain and suffering. Children must leave their birth families, often without their approval, because mommy and/or daddy can no longer or should no longer be their primary care provider. Although state agencies are responsible for protecting abused and neglected children, they are no substitute for a permanent, loving family.

The statistics are alarming. More than 119,000 children are in need of forever families. These waiting children are creative, intelligent, and filled with hopes and dreams, yet their futures are uncertain. Every child deserves and is entitled to a permanent loving home and family. Each year, thousands of men and women of all ages and colors choose to be the light in the life of a foster child by adopting them.

Daphine Reeves shares her family's adoption experience in this wonderful, detailed book. This book helps guide potential moms and dads through the maze of adoption. Mrs. Reeves serves as a cheerleader and encourages those who wish to adopt not to give up. She explains where families might experience delays; how they can access vital services and supports to ensure that their new families thrive; and how adoptive families can serve as advocates for their children.

If you have ever wondered if you should adopt from the U.S. foster care system, Mrs. Reeves and I would say a resounding "Yes!" You will experience joy, pain and all other emotions in between. It is an experience worth its weight in gold. Most importantly, the positive impact that you will make in the life of a child is priceless.

When I think about adoption, I envision a quilt. The quilt is built from different pieces of cloth. The fabrics often come in different shapes, sizes, and designs. Each section originated from coats, dresses and scarves. Carefully stitched together it becomes a work of art, a story to share with others.

Courteney Anne Holden
Executive Director, Voice for Adoption

1

Understanding Adoption

The journey of a thousand miles must begin with a single step.

—Chinese Proverb

When I was a young girl, I always *knew* I would have two children. My husband Dirk always dreamed of having a wife and children and growing old with them. Later their grandchildren would surround them with love. Many people share this dream of being part of a family that consists of adults and children. Many adults, whether couples or singles, long to conceive and raise children.

We were married three years before having our first child. I had a normal pregnancy and during my third trimester, we began decorating the baby's nursery. In August 1993, our lives were changed forever when our little girl was born. I did not know then, however, that this baby would be the only child to whom I would ever give birth.

When Morgan was three years old, we began talking of having a second child. Again, I became pregnant quickly and we were quite thrilled. However, at the end of the first trimester, we found out during a routine sonogram that we had miscarried. We dealt with the resultant pain and anger as best we could and life went on.

A year later, we had another miscarriage. The doctor performed many tests to see if I had Lupus, or another disease that may have caused two miscarriages. The doctor was perplexed when he found no obvious reason for our difficulties. We found out at this time that one in three pregnancies in America results in a miscarriage—a number that shocked and astounded us.

We started to wonder if it just was not our fate to have another child. A year or so later, we talked of possibly adopting a child. Neither of us truly believed we could adopt because we assumed that an adoption would require a huge financial commitment. Dirk was quite serious about his willingness to adopt, but I was not ready to give up on having a child born to us. The subject of having a second child faded away for a five-year period.

In July 2002, we had a third miscarriage. Our family members advised us to give up on having another child. "Just be happy with the one you have," they said. We tried again to have a child in early 2003, but never conceived. One morning in July of that year, before I left for work, Dirk said again that maybe it was best for us to adopt our second child. I didn't take those words to heart because I believed that we would never be able to afford to adopt.

As I was driving into work, my mind was filled with thoughts of happiness. I started thanking God for the wonderful husband He had given me. I thanked God for our sweet daughter. Moreover, I thanked Him for the many other ways in which we have been blessed. Unexpectedly, I began to cry. I was confused as to what was happening with me, as this was something that I had never before experienced. In the midst of feeling so grateful for what I did have, I experienced a deep sadness.

The sadness that I felt was the emptiness of not having another child. At that moment, I decided that I would indeed like to adopt a child. It was suddenly clear to me that adoption would be the way to complete our family and to fulfill our childhood dreams.

I shared my thoughts with Dirk that morning by phone. I said that I wanted to move forward with looking into adoption. Dirk was more than willing to move forward.

We began by exploring many private adoption agencies listed on the Internet and by calling several of them. We narrowed our decision to a small handful of agencies. We soon realized, however, that we would have to take money from our savings to adopt from a private agency. Since private agencies are not supported with public funds, they often charge fees from $5,000 to more than $35,000 to assist in the adoption of a child. Taking the money from savings didn't matter, however, because we were committed to the idea of adoption.

As I researched the private adoption agencies, one person to whom I spoke asked if we had considered adopting from the state. I learned that the expenses involved in a state adoption would be much less than those involved in an adoption from a private agency. Adoption services through a public agency are usually free or available for a relatively modest fee, since the services are funded by state and/or federal taxes. We then agreed to check into possibilities with the State of Texas where we lived.

Our journey through foster adoption was about to begin.

Questions to Ask Yourself Before Adopting

Every person considering adoption needs to think carefully before committing themselves.

- Can I be at total peace with raising a child to whom I did not give birth?

- Can I love this child as if she or he were born to me?

- Do I have the time and patience to raise a child?

- How will having a child affect my free time?

- How is my relationship with myself as well as with my spouse (if there is a spouse)?

- Is my mate totally committed to adopting a child?

- Do I/we have the financial security to raise a child?

- During the adoption process, can I accept intrusions in my personal life by total strangers?

Honest answers to these questions are important to everyone involved. It would be catastrophic to adopt a child and bring that child into your home only to later realize that you did not thoroughly think through your decision to adopt.

This book's intent is not to discourage anyone from adopting a child, but to help you to very carefully consider all aspects of adoption. Once these questions have been completely considered, the potential adoptive parent(s) is/are ready to move forward with the journey to adopt a child.

What is Foster/Adoption?

There are many types of adoptions. However, the purpose of this book is to discuss adoptions from the state foster care systems.

A *foster/adopt arrangement* is a child placement in which birth parents' rights have been severed in court. Social workers place the child with specially trained foster parents who will work with and care for the child until they meet the state requirements to be able to adopt the child.

Contacting Your County or State Agency

Your first step toward pursuing a state adoption is to contact the appropriate county or state agency. Each state has its own name for the agency assigned to handle foster and adoptive children. In Texas, it is the Department of Family and Protective Services (DFPS), specifically the Child Protective Services (CPS) office. DFPS is the state agency in charge of the disposition of children who have lost their parents or who have been removed from their parents or families for any number of reasons.

That first call was what I needed to get a general overview of how state adoption works and the requirements involved in adopting from the state. I also learned that this would be a lengthy process—usually a wait of at least nine months to adopt a child. I learned about the state's website that contained much more information about the process and the children waiting for families.

It is common for families to foster a child before deciding to adopt him or her. Often, a child being fostered is not yet legally free to adopt. This means that the child's parent(s)' rights have not been terminated nor voluntarily relinquished. In this scenario, the foster parent(s) take a chance that the child may be re-unified with his or her biological parent(s).

Note: The primary goal of CPS (and similar agencies in every state) is to return children to their biological families if the home situation can be resolved. CPS is not in the business of finding children for adoptive parents, but rather finding homes for children in need—whether for short-term or long-term fostering or for adoption.

At first, we did not want to accept a child into our home who was not already legally free to adopt. We were not interested in fostering a child for months or years, only to have him/her taken away. Prospective parents do have the option of refusing to foster, though it greatly reduces the chances of finding a child to adopt. Accepting only a child who was already legally free was our choice. Later we decided to not just accept a child who was legally free for adoption, but to help any child that was a healthy toddler.

Where to Turn For Help

While exploring the website for the State of Texas, we found an agency that partners with the state. This agency is called One Church, One Child (OCOC). We had a choice to work directly with the state, but due to the limited workers and their caseloads, we were told that most of the time, the process to be approved by the state could be sped along by working with an agency that is in partnership with the state. There are many agencies and groups that will help potential foster or adoptive parents. We chose OCOC and contacted the agency to find out more about the organization and what was required to adopt a child.

The first requirement was to register for the Parent Resource for Information Development Education classes, called PRIDE for short. OCOC also schedules a meeting with prospective parents to get to know them better before accepting them as "clients". We gave OCOC permission to run abuse/neglect and criminal background checks. Soon afterwards, we were contacted and told we could begin our classes in August.

Parents who work with the state are usually asked to meet with the state's social workers for similar reasons. Likewise, they usually have criminal background checks. Each state has its own requirements.

What Age Child is Best for You?

As we continued with OCOC, we talked about the child we wanted. We were not wrapped up in the idea of adopting an infant, as many families are. Our desire from the beginning was to adopt a toddler.

Knowing the age that will be the best fit for your family is crucial not only for you, but for the child as well. If you are a first-time parent, you may be interested in adopting an infant rather than a toddler or an older child. You may want to experience the newborn stages from the beginning with your child.

Some first-time parents in the beginning look forward to hearing their baby cry. And, even early morning feedings are exciting with a new baby. New parents long to see their infant grow through each stage of life. These parents look forward to the developmental milestones of a new life such as learning to sit up, crawling for the first time, attempting to talk, taking those hesitant first steps, and learning to say, "I love you, Mommy. I love you, Daddy."

There is nothing wrong with setting your mind on adopting an infant. Children require a lot of love, time, and devotion at any age. Realistically, though, there is always more of these required in raising an infant. You must realize that many other people are also determined to find a newborn. The waiting time for an infant is usually much greater than the waiting time for an older child.

Whether you are a first-time parent or an old pro, you may have the desire to adopt a toddler or an older child. Many of the children who are waiting for permanent homes are toddlers or older children. The demand for parents for toddlers and older children is tremendous in many states. Due to this abundance of older children, some states offer special tax breaks and/or other incentives for parents adopting them. These states offer monthly stipends and/or free college tuition through the state university system. Families adopting such children may also be eligible for tax credits on their federal and/or state income tax. Some families may have up to five years to use this credit. For more information, visit the North American Council on Adoptable Children website at www.nacac.org.

Preparing Other Children in the Family

Discussing the idea of adding to the family through adoption can be exciting, and, at the same time, frightening for children currently in the home. It is important to ask the child(ren)'s feelings regarding adding a new member to the family. Though the final decision to adopt is not necessarily left up to the child, it is crucial to get his/her input.

One who has been the only child for several years may not be open to the idea of adding a sibling to the family. An only child may feel that another child may take his/her place. She may even lose her sense of security by thinking that another child in the family will take attention from her. Children in larger families may not welcome another child or may see this child as an intrusion into an existing whirlwind of activity.

Conversely, a child could be bursting with excitement because he or she is going to have a sibling. Being the only child may not have been as much fun as having a little brother or sister. Many children in larger families like that big family "feel" and have a "more-the-merrier" attitude.

Deciding the Race or Ethnicity of the Child

Our ideal child would be a girl, two or three years old, and possibly of a mixed racial heritage. Her race was not important, however, but we had something to offer a child of mixed race since I am an African-American and Dirk is Anglo-American. We believed we could offer such a child an opportunity to maintain her mixed racial heritages.

Determining the race of the child you want to adopt is crucial. The decision will affect the lives of parents and children in many ways. While race cannot legally be considered a factor by the State when adopting, there are practical considerations involved.

Typically, many more minority children rather than Caucasian children are waiting to be adopted. African-American children lead the way numerically, but Hispanic and Asian children are also in great numbers, plus others of various minorities.

Usually, more Caucasian families adopt than minority families. This fact means that the numerical gap tends to widen between the races of children waiting for adoption. This can be to the advantage of a family who wants a minority child, as the waiting list is much shorter. Many states, and the federal government, will often classify a minority child (particularly older children or siblings adopted as a group to one family) as a child with special needs and will offer financial incentives to families who adopt them.

If you adopt a child of a race different from your own, you may be looked at by the public as something of an oddity. If you choose to adopt a child of a different race, you should ask yourself many questions before making this decision.

Can you deal with the attitudes of others? Friends and family members may voice opinions about other races that you never heard or expected from them before. If your family objects to you adopting a child of another race, can you have a distant relationship with that part of the family? How will you explain to your child the rejection of your family members?

Do you live by or associate with a diverse group of people, including those of the child's race? If not, would you be willing to move or be involved with a more diverse group if it may help your child? You may have thought of these questions already. However, if you find that it is difficult to answer these questions honestly and feel secure in your answers, you may want to reconsider your decision to adopt a child of another race.

Talking to the Extended Family and Friends

Within a few days of deciding to proceed with our journey to adopt, we began telling our extended family and friends. Almost everyone was genuinely happy for us. Almost everyone who knew us knew how much we had desired for years to have another child. We felt quite encouraged.

Family and friends wanted weekly updates from the time we began our PRIDE classes. We saw how our loved ones shared in our excitement and happiness and wanted to be involved in any way possible. However, we also had a few family members who were happy for us, but who also worried for us. They asked if we were really ready and prepared to adopt a child. They even questioned why we wanted to adopt a toddler instead of an infant. We sometimes found it difficult to talk to the family members who were constantly worrying about our decision to go forward.

For many people, talking to extended family members and friends about the decision to adopt may be harder than talking to the children in the home. They will ask many questions such as why, when, and where from. They will want to know your reasons for choosing to adopt. Others may ask how you will be able to do this. Most extended family members and friends will ask out of their love and concern. Family and friends who have not already considered adopting a child often think of the negative stories and myths about adoption. You may hear some of the following:

1. All children in the system have problems of one kind or another.

Most children who are in the state system have had problems that they have had to deal with such as abuse, neglect, and medical issues. How they dealt with those problems and how much these issues affect their lives presently varies from case to case. Given the proper care and love, they can all flourish and thrive. All children, whether they are wards of the state or your biological children, need to feel loved as well as safe and secure in their environment.

2. You will foster for many years before you actually get to adopt from the state.

The criteria your family decided on when you decided to adopt can have a major effect on the time you spend while waiting to adopt. If you want only to adopt a Caucasian infant with no medical issues, then you may wait for some time before the proper child comes along. If you are willing to adopt a minority child four years of age or older, then your duration can be shortened quite a bit. More minority children and more older children are in the system and many of them are legally free to be adopted right away.

3. You will have a very hard time raising a child out of the state system.

Raising any child, whether adopted or your biological child, is difficult. Only those persons who have never raised children think otherwise. Yes, you will take extra steps in working with the state; however, the process does not have to be a nightmare. If you are fostering a child while waiting for an adoption there is paperwork each month, but it is not usually prohibitive. Once you have adopted a child, the state is no longer involved, as you are the legal parent of the child.

4. By adopting a child from the state, you'll never know how she or he will turn out.

This time, we have to give this point to the "doubters." True, you won't know how the child will turn out. Even as you raise your biological child, you really will not know what he or she will eventually turn out to be.

The question, "What will my child be like when she grows up?" is a valid one whether you gave birth to the child or if you adopted the child. All children deserve a fair chance to prove their potential in life without being negatively typecast because of the circumstances of their birth. You, as the parent(s), should do the best job that that you possibly can in raising your child. (The Bible is full of child-rearing wisdom such as *"Train up a child in the way he should go, and when he is old he will not depart from it."*—Proverbs 22:6)

Equip Yourself with Patience, Perseverance, and Prayer

Once you have made the decision to adopt, you will need much patience, constant perseverance, and daily prayer. Making the decision to adopt is not an easy choice, but the journey ahead toward bringing your child home will test you in ways that you have never experienced before! There will be days when you will ask yourself if it is worth it. Then, there will be other days that you feel that you will never see the happy ending that you envision. Some days you will be completely drained mentally, emotionally, and physically.

Throughout the adoption process, your patience will be tested on a regular basis. Most potential parents experience several times where they are waiting for someone else to do something before their case will move on to the next step. Paperwork needs to be processed, files have to be assembled and read, and phone calls have to be made. These are things that the parent(s)-to-be have little or no control over. The system moves very slowly at times and it seems that one of those times is when you are trying to adopt a child.

As you go through the adoption process, you will have to persevere through many arduous tasks. Some things that are required may seem petty to you, but those who refuse the tasks or who dawdle in their completion fall out of the system. Keep in mind that a reason exists for each request.

With all the required paperwork that you have to fill out and return, you have to continue to tell yourself that the information is being collected to seek out the best possible family for the child. Oftentimes, many people who complete the PRIDE training never complete the required paperwork. Though they all had the hope and desire to foster or adopt children, they never obtained their license because they just got lost in the paperwork. They did not have enough desire or "stick-to-itiveness" to persevere to the end.

Last, but not least, prayer is also a vital tool that will sustain you during the vast amount of work you encounter during your adoption journey. Pray specifically for what you desire in the end. Ask for your family and friends to pray for you and your family. Pray for the child whom you wait for. Most of all believe and have faith that your prayers will be answered.

More Things to Consider Before Adopting

- Bringing your child home will not happen overnight. Patience will be necessary in waiting through the long months of preparation and training and more preparation.

- You will be required to share very private and personal things about your childhood as well as your adult life.

- Your life will seem to be on a roller coaster (very possibly for a lengthy time).

As you may begin to understand now, adoption involves a lot of decisions and hard choices. However, for the family that desires a child, it could be the best thing to ever happen to them.

2

Initial Steps in Adopting from the State

"Of journeying the benefits are many; the freshness it brings to the heart, the seeing and hearing of marvelous things..."

—Sheikh Muslih-uddin Sa'di Shirazi, 1184-1291, Persian poet

The first chapter discussed the various types of adoption and posed some questions you may want to consider before going forward. This chapter explains how to begin moving forward in your journey to adopt through your state's foster/adoptive system.

Visit Your State's Adoption Website

You can find much information on your state's website for their foster/adoption program. General information typically answers many of your questions.

Most state websites educate you on that state's process for state adoption. Some websites inform you of the general requirements in your state to adopt a child through its system.

Typically, a list of frequently asked questions (FAQs) are included to assist you. Moreover, many states offer photos of the children who are waiting to be adopted. Some states offer a list of private agencies that are in partnership with the state, as well, if you choose to go the private agency route. Visiting your state's website could be the smartest move you can make from the beginning.

When we were first told about our state's adoption website, we could not stay away from it. Looking at the children that were (and still are) waiting for a home was heartbreaking. We learned much in a short time by fully exploring the website. This time of learning also became very enlightening for our 10-year old daughter. She sat with us to look at the photos of the waiting children. She even chose a couple of children whom she wanted us to consider adopting.

We saw pictures of the same children over and over. Now, more than a year later, some of these children are still waiting. We often wonder what will become of those children who continue to wait for permanent homes.

See Appendix A for a list of each state's adoption website.

Call the Appropriate State Agency Office

Most state agency offices can also be quite helpful. If you have visited the state's website and still have more questions, you can usually contact your local county or state agency and speak to a placement worker. More than likely, you will receive the same information that is posted on the state's website. However, talking to a real person can sometimes bring you more security in the decision that you are making to adopt a child from the state. The placement worker may also be able to tell you where to attend an informational meeting.

Attend an Informational Meeting

You may be required to attend an informational meeting or you may choose to do so on your own. Many counties conduct informational meetings several times a month in varying locations. You can choose to attend a meeting that is convenient to you and fits your schedule.

The informational meeting describes the requirements of becoming a foster or adoptive parent in detail. You may have an opportunity to see photos of children waiting to be adopted. You will definitely have the opportunity to ask questions. If you are ready to move forward after the meeting, you may be asked to begin completing some basic paperwork. In addition, you will be asked to give the state permission to run a criminal and abuse/neglect background check on the family members living in your home. For many people, this meeting is the first real step of their journey.

Talk With Others Who Have Adopted From the State

Many people have added to their families by adopting through the state system. There are all types of people who adopt children—married couples and single people, some younger and some older. Many of these will tell you how wonderful their adoption journey was for them. Others will tell you the nightmare that they cannot forget. As with anything, adoption can sometimes fail.

A good way to find parents who have adopted from the state is to join or visit a local support group. Many families will share their stories with you. In fact, most adoptive parents will be happy to answer any questions that you may have.

It is always encouraging to hear of successful stories. As you are hearing another family's success story, it is easy to put yourself where they are. It may be a little easier to imagine that you could be telling your success story in the near future. Keep in mind that every adoption journey is different.

Know the Statistics

The following statistics are taken from data collected by the Adoption and Foster Care Analysis and Reporting System (AFCARS) and released by the U.S. Department of Health and Human Services in March 2003.

*Children in state foster care and waiting for adoption

Approximately 532,000 children were in foster care in the U.S. in 2002. Of these, 126,000 were eligible for immediate adoption.

*Age of children waiting to be adopted from state foster care

- 3% were less than one year old

- 32% were 1-5 years

- 30% were 6-10 years

- 29% were 11-15 years

- 5% were 16-18 years old

*Gender of children waiting to be adopted

- 53% are male

- 47% are female

*Race/ethnicity of children to be adopted

Approximately 65% of children waiting to be adopted are of minority backgrounds—

- 42% are black

- 13% are Hispanic

- 2% are American Indian

- Less than 1% are Asian/Pacific Islander

- 4% are unknown/unable to determine

- 3% are two or more races

Thirty-four percent are Caucasian.

*Children in foster care that had their parental rights terminated

67,000 children.

*Months it takes after termination of parental rights for the children to be adopted

- 4% of children have waited less than a month

- 18% of the children waited 1–5 months

- 27% waited 6–11 months

- 19% waited 12–17 months

- 11% waited 18–23 months

- 7% waited 24–29 months

- 4% waited 30–35 months

- 6% waited 3 to 4 years

- 2% waited 5 or more years

*Single adults seeking to adopt

Thirty percent of children adopted from foster care are adopted by a single parent.

Single-parent adoption is becoming more and more common. Many years ago, agencies would not consider unmarried men or women as prospective adoptive parents. Due to the increased divorce rate and more households becoming one-parent households, most agencies now more frequently consider single-parent adoption.

General Requirements to Foster/Adopt

Some states vary in their general requirements to foster/adopt. However, most states' requirements run along similar lines. Visit your state's website to find out their general requirements. These are the basic requirements that most states require:

1. Be of at least 21 years of age

2. Be financially stable and responsible

3. Complete an application

4. Share information regarding background and lifestyle

5. Provide references from relatives and non-relatives

6. Show proof of marriage and/or divorce, as applicable

7. Agree to a home study, which includes interviews with all household members

8. Be willing to get fire and health inspections of your home and meet any requirements to reach a passing grade

9. Consent to a criminal history background check and an abuse check (this requirement is for all adults in the household)

10. Attend training classes to learn about children who have been abused and neglected.

Complete the Application

In most states, an application is required. The application asks questions that are relatively easy to answer pertaining to you and your family. It requires answers to the following:

- Provide your name, address, phone number, social security number, driver's license number, and birth date

- Include directions to your home

- Describe the type of child(ren) you are interested in adopting along with age range, sex, and race/ethnicity.

- Include marital information along with date of marriage and place of marriage if applicable

- Include information on divorce if applicable

- List other household members' names, genders, relationship to you, dates of birth, and their health issues, if any

- List any children living outside the household

- Provide employment and annual income information

- Include household expenses

- List assets such as stocks, bonds, savings, investments, etc.

- List the names and addresses of four to five references including phone numbers. (Your state may solicit information from these references regarding their opinions of your ability to parent a child, care for a child in your home, provide emotional support, etc.)

The journey is lengthy, but if you commit yourself from the beginning, you can succeed!

3

Getting Your Home Approved

"When we are sure that we are on the right road....
We cannot take more than one step at a time..."

Orison Swett Marden, 1850–1924,
American Author and Founder of *Success* Magazine

After reviewing the initial steps involved with adopting from your state, it may not seem like much is involved. Adoption, though, requires much dedication and hard work. When you adopt from the state, you can either work directly with your state or with an agency that is in partnership with your state.

Often working with such an agency can help get you licensed for adoption sooner than working with your state. This is based on the fact that most states do not have enough workers, and, thus, cannot work as quickly as a private agency. The caseload for a state worker is sometimes quite great and often the state worker is very involved in dealing with day-to-day issues instead of working toward getting more families licensed.

Note: If your state's website does not list the private agencies that are in partnership with the state, be sure to ask if there are any such agencies.

Parenting Classes

Most states require you to take a parenting class to be licensed. The classes are generally another resource to help you make an informed decision about adopting. Even with the great amount of adoption information on the Internet, in magazine articles and in books, and from support groups, there is nothing available to prepare you more than the licensing classes themselves.

Parenting classes are a thorough guide as to exactly what you are getting yourself into. You will learn about the types of children who are waiting in the state foster care system. You will learn about all aspects of these children, including the severest of problems. Many of these children have been exposed to things that would rattle adults to the core. Many have been forced to cope with situations they are not equipped for. The results of this exposure and abuse can be quite dramatic. First-time parents or parents who have never dealt with abuse issues need these classes to be prepared for the upcoming trials and problems.

The classes will equip you with the knowledge you need to see if you are truly prepared to be a foster/adoptive parent. During training you will learn that becoming an adoptive parent without a training program is like buying a suit or a dress in a store without trying it on.

We were both excited as we drove to our first PRIDE class. We were the first people to arrive. We even arrived before the instructor! We were a bit nervous, yet excited at the same time. My stomach was in knots because I realized this was a very big step toward adopting our child.

In the first class meeting, we discussed many topics. It seemed somewhat overwhelming to take in so much information during just one class. The PRIDE course is designed to train both potential adoptive parents and future foster parents. Our class consisted of four couples and four single women.

A key point that the instructors made clear early in our training was that the state's main goal is always to reunite the child with his or her biological parent(s), if possible. This comment was a bit frightening to us since our goal was to adopt. However, we were appreciative of the honest comments and answers that our instructors gave.

After hearing all the information in the first training class, we found ourselves even more committed. We were concerned by some issues discussed in class, but we still wanted to proceed. We wondered if any of our classmates would be scared away, but everyone returned to the next class the following week.

Taking this course was a great experience for us. Our instructors were both informative and entertaining. We met some interesting people in our class. Listening to our classmates' stories was educational and informative. Each of us had our own reasons for participating in the class.

Some couples could not conceive children of their own and wanted to adopt. One couple had grown children that had left home and they wanted to foster a child. Single women in the class wanted a child and felt that they could be a blessing to a child even as a single parent.

Each week we received a thick bundle of paperwork that needed to be returned as soon as possible. Despite this, we were definitely ready to be finished and move on to the next step.

Whether you receive your paperwork on a weekly basis or you get it all at once, as some other parents say happened to them, it seems endless. Completing this paperwork may include an activity to help you think of a particular situation that could arise with your future child. You are placed in many scenarios and asked to role-play. For example, what do you do if your child becomes withdrawn? How would you handle a disobedient child? What about a child who exhibits signs of anxiety or stress? What do you do if your child shows an interest in the opposite sex at an early age (perhaps a *very* early age)? The answers you provide will help the state to determine your suitability as a potential parent.

Other homework includes answering numerous questions about your past and present life. What was your family life like as you were growing up? How did your family relate together during times of stress? Who first told you about "the birds and the bees" and what did this person say? How do you relate to your parents and siblings now? You are asked to answer many questions about your sex life, both past and present. These types of questions are indeed necessary, because, some of the children in the state system have been exposed to inappropriate things regarding sex and sexual activity and there is always a possibility that some delicate situations could arise. Your personal life experiences certainly influence the way you handle difficult issues.

Of course, there is also a certain amount of paperwork regarding mundane information such as home address and phone number(s), work history, financial situation, etc.

When we were first given a stack of paperwork to be completed and returned, we did not think it was asking too terribly much of us. However, after completing the first stack of paperwork over several hours time, we knew this was not going to be easy.

We continued to encourage ourselves by saying that this was for our child that was to come. We told each other that this was good that we had to be thorough in completing so much paperwork that told about us, our family, our extended family members, our neighbors, and so on.

Our class instructors told us that each piece of paper that we completed would provide valuable input about us and that someone would actually read every answer we submitted. Our answers were to be considered a big factor in the decision to grant our license.

We learned that in many cases, prospective foster/adoptive parents are not approved by the state because they just do not take the time to complete the requested paperwork. This was definitely not going to be the case with us. We agreed that each time we showed up for our class, we would turn in all of our paperwork as requested.

The sheer volume of paper was daunting. By determining to turn in all of the paperwork each week, we put a lot more pressure on ourselves. In the end, though, it allowed us to keep from facing a mountain of paper when the class was done. We had to work on the questions almost daily to have them completed by the deadline, but we were able to get it done. By never letting it build up, we were able to keep it under control and manageable.

The classes themselves were wonderful, though. We learned so much each time we went to class. In fact, we looked forward each week to seeing what we would learn next. The program to become a foster/adoptive parent takes a lot of your time and energy, yet you aren't certain of the outcome. The demands on the prospective parents are great, but there is good reason for the exacting lessons. Having knowledgeable parents, ready to face the coming trials, keeps children from further disruptions, and protects the whole family from an unhappy experience. We learned things that we needed to know to be better prepared for the changes ahead.

The day we completed our last class was a big day for all the participants. We had agreed to meet an hour earlier than normal to have breakfast together. Everyone brought something to share with the others. There was, however, still a lot to be accomplished during this last training class. The agenda consisted of water safety training, CPR/First Aid Certification, a tuberculosis test, and previous foster/adoptive parents came and spoke about their experiences. We were fortunate in this, though. Most classes do not offer to provide for all of these tests and specialized training in one sitting. Typically, students have to arrange for these themselves. Yet, by four-o'clock that afternoon, our training was officially over and we received our certificates stating that we had successfully completed the training!

The most memorable thing about hearing from other adoptive parents was learning of their experiences with state adoption. One parent's experience was not totally positive, but we were still encouraged by it. We knew that one day we would be telling our own story and encouraging others as well. Little did we know that it would happen for us so quickly.

Health and Fire Inspections

One requirement before arranging for our home study was to have our home inspected by the fire and health departments. In many areas, these are provided free of charge for potential adoptive parents. Contact your local health and fire departments to see if they charge for these inspections.

I called our local health and fire departments to inquire what we needed to do to get an inspection. Surprisingly, I was able to set up both inspections for the following day. We had a list of items the inspectors would be looking for and spent some time that evening double-checking our home. The time was well spent as we passed both inspections with no problems.

We could not wait to get back to class the following Saturday and tell everyone about the accomplishments that we had achieved during the week. We wanted the class to know for a couple of reasons. First, we wanted them to know just how excited we were that we had gotten over the first hurdle. Second, we wanted to let the others know that it was painless to make the call and get things rolling. The class was so excited for us after we shared the story about our inspections.

Others were encouraged to make their inspection phone calls as well. I thought at the time, "If only the rest of this journey would go as smoothly as these inspections did, everything would be great."

Health Inspection

The health inspection can seem intimidating if you are not sure what it consists of. Your city or county health department typically conducts this inspection. Be sure to call well in advance to see if they have a backlog of homes to inspect. Some areas are able to inspect homes right away, but others may have a lengthy waiting list.

Generally, you can get a checklist from your class instructor or the health department before the inspection is scheduled. The checklist is typically a "yes" or "no" answer sheet. Although each state or municipality may differ in what is on their checklist, here are a few things that may be asked:

- Does the home have hot and cold running water?

- Is the home kept clean and free of hazards to children?

- Are the bathrooms kept clean?

- If there is a glass door, is it clearly marked at a child's level to prevent accidents?

- Are there childproof latches on all cabinet doors where there are chemicals?

- Does the plumbing appear to be in good working condition?

- Are perishable foods refrigerated or stored properly in other ways?

- Is there at least one toilet, lavatory, and bathtub or shower inside the home?

- Is the yard kept free of garbage and trash?

- Are medicines stored in such a way so that children cannot get to them?

If you do get a checklist in advance, take advantage of the opportunity to get things ship shape before the inspector arrives. Forcing the inspector to check over an obviously unprepared home will not make them happy. They will probably feel the need to check even closer when they return, as well, to make sure things were corrected properly.

Fire Inspection

Your city fire department typically performs the fire inspection. Your class instructor may be able to give you a checklist before the inspection so that you can see all the areas that are covered. Although this is not a complete list of what the inspection includes, it should help to give you an idea:

- Are there at least two unblocked exits to the outside from the home?

- Does the electrical wiring system appear to be in good repair?

- Do the electrical outlets in public rooms and rooms used by children have childproof covers?

- Are space heaters enclosed to prevent children from burning themselves?

- Are all lighters and matches kept out of the reach of children?

- If present, is paint kept in tightly closed metal containers?

- Are flammable liquids stored in safety cans and kept away from heat and children?

- Is there an operable #5 pound dry chemical fire extinguisher available for use in the kitchen? Is the expiration date clearly visible?

- Are fire drills practiced regularly?

- Is there a way to alert the family of a fire in the house (alarm, bell, etc)?

- If the home is two-story, is there a ladder to climb out of an upper-floor window, if needed?

Such an inspection may help to prepare to keep your family safe in ways that you never before considered.

The Home Study

Each state and Washington D.C. requires all parents who want to adopt to participate in a home study. This is a time to gather information about the family that will help the agency to match the proper child to the proper family, and to get a complete evaluation of the adoptive family. The home study often causes some anxiety for prospective parents, who are concerned about being rejected as unsuitable. It may be helpful to remember that the state understands that the parents are real parents with real imperfections. The specific requirements of the states vary somewhat and it may be helpful for you to obtain specific information about the requirements of your state before proceeding.

A licensed social worker conducts your home study after you complete and submit all of your paperwork.

We waited a couple of weeks after completing our PRIDE training and had still not heard whether our home study had been scheduled. We called one of our class instructors who said we would soon get a call to set it up.

Before we knew it, the whole month of September had come and gone. We still had not received a phone call to schedule our home study. We called our instructor, feeling a bit discouraged that we had already waited a month for a phone call. I questioned why we had worked so hard to get all of our paperwork submitted in a timely manner just to have to wait on the home study.

The instructor listened to my discouragement and then asked us to continue to be patient. Something in the instructor's voice really settled my thoughts. I hung up the phone and thought to myself that there must be a very good reason why it was taking so long just for our file to be passed along and a call to be made to set up this home study. We have been told since that others have their study done almost immediately after requesting it. We just had some bad luck in this case.

In mid-October, we received the long awaited phone call for our home study to be performed. It was scheduled for the last week in October. We learned that the home study usually consists of two meetings. The woman who would do the home study wanted to know, however, if we would be interested in trying to do the home study all at once. We had in our minds from the beginning that we would not be the reason for any hold ups with this adoption. We happily agreed to do the home study in one visit instead of two.

The social worker arrived at our home at 1:45 in the afternoon and left at 8:25 that night. The study was a general overview of many of the questions that we had already answered. We were interviewed both separately and together. The social worker also interviewed our daughter without Mom and Dad present to "feed" her answers. She asked us questions regarding our childhood, our married life, our daughter's life, the rules in our house, our religion, our finances, our employment, and our education.

The home study itself was not really a hard physical process, although as a result of answering so many questions, we were left feeling emotionally drained. When the home study was completed, we breathed a heavy sigh of relief. The home study was the final part of the process for us to be approved by the state. Now all we had to do was wait for the state to call us and let us know if we were approved.

The social worker's job was to inspect our house physically, but that was only a small part of what she was looking for. After all, the fire and health departments had already inspected us. She was only confirming their findings. She was not looking to see if we kept our home meticulously clean. Instead, she was more concerned about the general state of our home. Did it look cared for? The worker's primary concern was that the home was safe and comforting for the child. Most importantly, she was there to get a "feel" about us as individuals and as a family. Her job was to find out if we seemed to be telling the truth when we answered her questions.

After her visit, she would make a recommendation to her supervisor, who could overrule her, but who typically agrees with the findings of the home study. This was the last and most important step to obtaining our license.

The home study can be quite costly if you choose not to adopt through the foster care system. The fees involved for a home study can range from $1,000 to $3,000. Normally, if you are adopting a child from the state, there is no charge for the home study or at least a greatly reduced fee. The state absorbs this cost. However, if there is a fee, it is typically between $300 and $500.

Note: Once your adoption is finalized, you may even be reimbursed this fee.

The Home Study Interview(s)

During the home study, each person living in the home is interviewed individually and as a group. You will be asked how you came to the decision to adopt a child. You will be asked what type of child is the ideal fit for your family, about your marriage relationship (positives and negatives), your childhood, past and present relationship with your parents and your siblings (if any). There are questions asked about your friends and neighbors. You will even answer questions about your pet(s). You will be asked about your employment and education. Typically, you will be asked about your religion as well.

The social worker will also ask about your parenting skills and type of discipline and/or punishment you use in your home. You will be asked how you handle stress in your life. If you have adult children living outside the home, they may be interviewed as well. The interviews are a lengthy process. More than one interview may be scheduled with your family.

Documents Needed in the Home Study

Each state has a different list of the documents required as part of a home study. Depending on the agency and/or state, some of these documents may be required for submission before your home study is scheduled. The prospective parents can expect to provide the following documents and possibly a few more that are not listed:

- Certified copy of Marriage certificate (if applicable)

- Certified copy of Divorce decree(s) (if applicable)

- Certified copy of Birth certificates for children already living in the home

- Medical reports completed within the last year for all members of the household

- Income verification (W-2 form or income tax forms)

- State-mandated fingerprint clearances

- Proof of health insurance to cover the child

- Proof of life insurance to cover the child

- Proof of mortgage or rent payment

- Statement of current assets, including savings accounts, money market accounts, mutual funds, stocks, bonds, etc.

- Approved home health inspection

- Approved home fire inspection

- Photos of all members of the household

- Photos of the home

- Written personal references

Personal References

You may also be asked to provide personal references. These might be a relative, an employer, a co-worker, a close friend, a neighbor, or your pastor. This information may be requested before your actual home study interview is conducted. You should list people who have known you for several years.

It is important to furnish the social worker reliable references who will reply to a letter mailed to them or respond to a telephone interview if they are contacted by a state employee. It is imperative that your personal references respond in whatever way that is requested of them. If a questionnaire letter is mailed to your references, a self-addressed, postage-paid envelope is typically included for them to return.

If a telephone interview is conducted instead and if your reference has to return a phone call, in most cases, the state will provide a toll-free number for your reference to call. The state attempts to make it easy for your references to respond. Lack of responses, or negative responses, can lead to your application for adoption being denied.

The references are asked questions about you, your life, and your lifestyle. It may be best to inform those people whom you have listed as references so that they are aware that they will be contacted by a state employee. It may also be a good idea to tell them how important this is to you that they respond promptly.

Though there is no part of the licensing process that is unimportant, it cannot be stressed enough how important the physical home environment is in having a family approved for adoption. The greatest, most loving family in the world will not be approved if they have an unsafe or unfit home environment.

Money is not the main issue. Owning (or buying) the home is not the issue either. Being able to provide a reasonably clean, safe, and loving environment is what this is all about. The potential parents do not have to own the home. It doesn't even have to be a "house" in the traditional sense of the word. The family could live in an apartment. As long as the child(ren) will be cared for in proper, safe conditions, the family should have to make only minor adjustments to get the home approved.

4

Awaiting that All-Important Call

"The journey a professional football team starts in training camp, thru the pre-season, the 16-game regular season, and finally the playoffs, is full of ups and downs...players get injured, teams often change strategies, and many events lead to the ultimate success...The bottom line is the team that wins the Super Bowl must overcome adversity, work hard, and keep their eye on the prize."

Bill Keller, Bill Keller Ministries and founder of LivePrayer.com

Now that you have completed the required paperwork, parenting classes, and the home study, you wait with anticipation for your child. To some people the waiting is the most agonizing period of all. Unfortunately, there is no way to determine how long your wait may be.

It is certainly okay to feel somewhat frustrated. However, remember that the worker responsible for getting your file/information pushed through to completion is working as hard as he or she can. Many people have to read and review all information related to your file. This is certainly a lengthy process because of all of the laborious reading and double-checking. Every piece of paper you have filled out is read and reviewed, often by several people.

Some people may wait a few weeks and others may wait several weeks or even several months. Be patient. Your state agency has not forgotten about you.

What to do While you Wait

• Read, Read, and Read

You can find mountains of reading material at your local library regarding adoption in general. Many parenting books can also be of help to you if you are a first-time parent. You may want to subscribe to a magazine that focuses on adoption. Some prospective parents may also enroll in parenting courses at their local community colleges, churches, or social organizations.

We checked out many books from our library regarding adoption. Most of them gave the same information pertaining to private adoptions. Some of them mentioned the option of adoption through the state, but we did not find information that could be considered a "guide" as to how to best navigate the system. We purchased books that we thought would be helpful to us. Moreover, we visited countless websites regarding state foster adoption.

• Join a Support Group

The social, emotional, and psychological support from other adoptive or prospective parents is usually quite positive. It can be a huge encouragement to listen and/or talk to others who have been where you are. Allowing a support group to be a part of your life during and after the adoption can be very valuable. These groups are not only informative, but they can be fun to participate in. Such groups often plan family activities.

We joined a support group soon after our home study was completed—quite a smart move. We found it very interesting to listen to other successful stories in our group. It was also encouraging listening to others who were still waiting for their child just as we were awaiting ours. We found that there seemed to be a special connection with everyone who attends. It seems like we were all comfortable in voicing our thoughts and concerns.

A support group can also offer extended training. Each time we meet, there is time allotted for ongoing training and information gathering. We also hear from professional speakers who guide us in some of the issues that we may encounter.

You will find that subjects vary and cover a wide range of topics. If your state requires you to undergo a certain amount of annual training to maintain your license, these sessions may count as training credits. The leader of the group or association should be able to tell you if this is the case.

• Keep a Journal

Journaling is a great way to record not only events as they happen, but also your feelings and hopes. In addition, journaling is also a form of therapy. Moreover, your recorded thoughts can be something you may want to share with your adopted child when he or she gets older. It can be beneficial to record even the tough times that you may be experiencing during your journey.

Keeping a journal during our journey was one of the best things that we could have done. It was therapeutic to record our thoughts as we progressed. We even had our daughter, Morgan, record an entry discussing her feelings about having a baby sister. Our journal is something that we have gone back and re-read several times throughout our journey. It is something that we will always read again and again. We plan for our adopted daughter to read it when she gets older.

• Prepare a Photo Album

If you are adopting a toddler or an older child, the agency may ask you to prepare a photo album. The album may include all household members, pets, and pictures of your home (inside and out). The album that you put together does not have to be fancy. The pictures you include will be far more important to the child than a fancy album. This may be asked of you to prepare the child ahead to meet you before your pre-placement visits begin with her/him. It could be a wonderful way for you to be presented to your child. Although, you will still be a stranger to the child on the first visit or so, it may help the child with her fears of talking to or meeting strangers.

The day that we were told that our family was chosen for our child, we were also informed that we needed a photo album to send to the child. We had the album compiled the next day! The album included many pictures of our family and of Sammy, our Bassett Hound. We also included pictures of the rooms in our home and pictures of the front and back of our home. We did not know when our presentation meeting was going to be scheduled, but we went ahead and packed the album in our car ahead of time! We knew that once the meeting was scheduled, we would already be prepared to give our album to our case-worker.

Eventually, the presentation meeting was set and the album was presented as well. The social workers were enthusiastic about the album and being able to provide it to the child.

- **Learn the process for adding your child(ren) to your insurance**

Under the Health Insurance Portability and Accountability Act of 1996 (HIPAA, for short), health insurance issuers must cover the insured person's adoptive child, including pre-existing conditions. The insurance company most likely will request written proof of adoption or foster child status to add your new child to the policy. The coverage for your adoptive child should be the same as any dependent added to your policy.

Check with your health administrator to get the new enrollment paperwork that you need. You should be able to add the child immediately upon the child's placement. If the child had Medicaid benefits prior to adoption and is considered a "special needs" adoption, then those benefits may continue.

Until researching information for this book, we did not know that our health insurance issuer must cover our adoptive child. In fact, we had no idea that this was a law. Within a week of us deciding to adopt, we contacted our insurance carrier to see if our adoptive child would be covered. We were told that our child would be covered, but not until the adoption was finalized. While writing this book, I called our insurance company again and was told that the child should have been added the day of our placement and that we did not have to wait until adoption was consummated. It is good to know what your child's rights are regarding insurance coverage.

- **Find a pediatrician**

While you are waiting for your child's placement in your home, find a reputable and competent pediatrician with whom you and your child will be comfortable. There are several ways to go about finding the right pediatrician. Your friends who are already parents may be able to refer you to the pediatrician their children see. You may also locate a pediatrician through the Internet. However you go about finding a doctor for your child, have a list of questions to ask when you make the initial call. What are the doctor's credentials? Is the doctor accepting new patients? How long does it take to get an appointment? Does the doctor accept your insurance provider? What are his/her normal office hours? What hospital does the doctor use? How are emergency calls handled?

We already had a pediatrician that we had used for ten years with our first daughter. Knowing that we already had a good, reputable doctor made things easy for us. When we spoke with our doctor's office regarding the adoption of our little girl, we wanted to see if our doctor was willing to accept a new patient. We were elated that we could have the same doctor for both of our girls.

- **Arrange to take time off from work**

When your child arrives home, you will probably feel the need to build a relationship with your child. You will want begin the bonding period immediately. Consider taking some time off to facilitate the process.

Under the Family and Medical Leave Act of 1993 (FMLA), employers must allow an eligible employee to take unpaid leave absences from their job when a child is born or adopted into the family. An eligible employee can take up to twelve weeks off without pay during any twelve-month period. FMLA also guarantees that mothers and fathers will be able to return to their same job and duties. Employers must be given a 30-day notice before the leave begins. You are an eligible employee if you have worked with your company for at least 12-months, you have worked for at least 1,250 hours for your employer during the 12-month period, and if you work for an employer who has 50 or more workers employed within 75 miles of their location. In addition, some employers may offer more generous benefits if you are taking time off to bond with your new child. For more information, check your employee handbook or talk to the human resources manager of your company.

We both work outside the home. We knew that we would want to take some time off to bond with our newest little girl. We informed our employers immediately after we started our training classes that we were adopting a child and would be taking time off. It was not a problem for either of us to take the time off once we brought our daughter home. Everything worked out wonderfully with us because we had given proper notice well ahead of time. We were able to have time at home to bond with our daughter and return to our jobs.

- **Explore child care options**

For some parents, the time to leave the job may be when the child is placed in their home. Other parents who want (or need) to return to work after adopting will want to be at peace with whoever becomes the childcare provider for their child. Finding a child-care facility can be hard to do.

No two child-care facilities are same, yet, they all have at least one thing in common. They think that you should choose their daycare because they will provide better care to your child than the daycare next door.

There are several ways that you can find a reputable daycare center. Ask your family and friends whose children attend daycare facilities about their feelings regarding the level of care at those facilities. If your search is through the yellow pages or by searching the Internet, ask the daycare center if it is possible for you to obtain references of parents whose children are currently enrolled in their facility. If they cannot or will not provide references, find another facility.

Have a list of questions that you want to know about the center itself and the care it provides. Some pertinent questions might be;

- Is the daycare licensed by the state to care for foster children? Many states require that foster children be placed in a facility that is inspected and licensed for such children. Placing the child(ren) in an unlicensed facility can result in their removal from the foster home.

- Does the center allow for unplanned visits? Most centers will offer you a tour of their facility any time. Visit several additional times unannounced if you were impressed by the daycare on the first visit. Spend time in the class where your child is likely to be. Observe the worker's interaction with the children. If the facility objects to your unannounced arrival and quiet observations, find another facility.

- What kind of meals and snacks are offered? Check this out for yourself. It is easy to make a menu sound good on paper. It is another thing entirely to make it taste and look good in person. Also find out if the menu is actually followed or is it just a "wish list".

- What is the ratio of caregivers to children? Are the caregivers watching too many children? Do they have the ability to keep an eye on all of them? This is especially important when dealing with children who have been physically or sexually abused. They can sometimes act out the part of the abuser on other children if they are not supervised properly.

- What is the disciplinary policy? Many states have a "non-violent" disciplinary policy they require their foster families to follow. Allowing a childcare facility to enforce a disciplinary action involving physical punishment (spanking hands or bottoms) can result in the state taking the child away from the foster family.

Take your time in choosing a child care facility. There are good daycare facilities, and, unfortunately, there are also bad ones to avoid.

If you choose a traditional babysitter for your child, this person may have to undergo an approval process from the state. Generally, the babysitter will be required to undergo a criminal background check, take several parenting classes, and become CPR and first aid certified. Some states may even require these caregivers to have home health and fire inspections.

We chose a reputable and reliable daycare facility for our new daughter and we were pleased with our choice.

It is easy to become discouraged while you are waiting for the state's call informing you that your family is approved to adopt a child. However, if you keep occupied doing most of the things listed above, you will be pleased that you used your "wait" time wisely!

5

The Call for Placement

We are at our very best, and we are happiest, when we are fully engaged in...the journey toward the goal...It makes everything else in life so wonderful, so worthwhile.

—Earl Nightingale, American Author and Motivator, 1921–1989

We were officially licensed in early December. Christmas and New Year's Day came and went, but we still had not received the offer for the right child. On January 5, the phone finally rang with the right offer. I received a call at work from our placement worker. She gave a brief profile of a child. She was a two-and-a-half year old, healthy child and she was legally free for adoption. The placement worker asked if we would be interested in having our family submitted as her new foster family and, eventually, her adoptive parents. I couldn't hang up the phone fast enough to call Dirk. Since this was the phone call that we had hoped and prayed for all these months, we accepted the offer right away for our family to be submitted for consideration.

When the placement worker finally calls you for an adoption placement, you may be willing to accept almost any child no matter what. You may feel as if you have waited long enough. Your mind may tell you that you cannot possibly wait for another placement call if you don't accept this one.

Do not be too quick to accept a child that you already suspect may not fit into your family. It might not only be a bad decision for your family, it could also be a devastating disruption for the child if you act on your emotions without proper forethought.

If your family has already made the decision of exactly what type of child will fit in your family and you feel at peace with it, don't accept the "wrong" placement no matter how wonderfully the child is presented to you over the phone. Moreover, do not expect that the first placement call is to be the child you have to accept. When you accept the adoption placement, you want to feel at peace and be confident with your decision.

General Information Given to Prospective Parents

In the initial phone call for the placement, the worker may only give limited information regarding the child. The information may be the child's gender, age, and race. Information given to you is limited so as to protect the child's privacy in case you do not accept the placement. (The state must protect the child's right to privacy. If you do not accept the child, his or her privacy is still fully protected.) You will also get a brief summary of the child's health. If the parents' rights have been terminated, this information will be shared with you. In addition, if the child is residing in a foster home, the placement worker will inform you of this also.

Questions to Ask Your Placement Worker

Placement workers try to fill you in as much as they are allowed to. Unfortunately, many things you may want to know about the child may not be mentioned.

It is a good idea to have your questions written down and kept near your telephone. Then, when the placement worker calls, you can get the information that you are seeking. Some common questions are;

- Why did the child come into the state's care?

- When did child come into the state's care?

- What is the child's medical condition? Does the child require any medications on a daily basis?

- How is the child's psychological condition? Has a formal psychological evaluation been performed?

- What is the child's developmental level?

- Is the child in any kind of therapy?

- If child is of school age, what grade is the child in?

- Does the child have any learning disabilities?

- Does the child have major negative habits (such as starting fires, urinating in inappropriate places, stealing, or uncontrollable screaming)?

- Does the child have any sexual experience (Considering the fact that many of these children have been abused in various ways, this is a valid question for even the youngest children)?

Although the placement worker is limited regarding information that can be shared with you until your family is chosen for the child, most of these commonly asked questions should be answerable.

The Selection Process

If you have spoken with the placement worker and have found nothing to make you give an immediate "no" to accepting a child, you will typically be given a day or so to respond with an answer regarding possible placement with your family.

If your family decides that you are interested in the child, then the placement worker submits your home study for consideration for the child. Normally, the state will try to find a handful of families to consider for each child. By doing this, the state can choose the best possible family for the child. Your home study is re-read by a staffing team of state workers who make the final decision. These people may include the child's caseworker and several different managers in the staffing team committee.

Remember—do not expect an overnight decision. You should be prepared to wait several weeks depending on how quickly the child needs to be placed. In some cases, the child could need to be placed immediately. In other cases, if the child is already in a loving foster home and the foster parents are okay with a slower transition for the child to leave, the decision to choose a family could be delayed.

Once the staffing team has read all of the submitted home studies for an adoptive placement, they then choose the family that they believe is best for the child. Everyone who is involved in the decision making for the child's adoptive family knows the child's life story and current situation. Once the decision is made, the families involved are informed of the results. If your family is selected, the social worker prepares the child's complete case file to be sent to you.

Things that the staffing team considers when selecting a family for a child are;

- A family that can provide a safe and secure environment for the child

- The duration and stability of the marriage and any former relationships

- A family commitment to adoption

- A family's ability to ask for and use outside help and resources and share issues that arise during placement with the case worker

- The prospective parent(s) medical history

- The prospective parent(s) adjustment to infertility, if applicable

- A family that is emotionally and physically able to parent the child until he/she reaches the age of adulthood

- A family that is financially stable

- A family that will provide appropriate care and seek community resources and services as the child may need

- A family that will provide proper education with the child's ability in mind

- A family that is accepting of the child's family and genetic history

- A family that will allow the child to continue sibling contact if siblings are not placed together and if such contact is in the child's best interests

- A family with children who are supportive of the plan to adopt

- A family that can be an advocate for the child and solve problems when they arise

Although this is not a complete list of what the staffing team looks for when choosing a family, these are some of the factors considered.

We waited several weeks to find out if we were to be selected as the right family for the little girl. On February 13, I arrived home first and began to unwind from a long day. Dirk picked up our daughter from school and they came home together. They walked into the room and handed me a card, a stuffed animal, and a bouquet of flowers. I smiled happily assuming that this was a Valentine's Day gift.

I opened the card. Written inside was, "Mom, you loved me before you even met me. Thank you for being the wonderful person you are. I love you already. Happy Valentine's Day. Love, Jae" (the name of the little girl we wanted to adopt). Earlier in the day, our placement worker had called Dirk at the office when she could not reach me first. Dirk knew we had been chosen as the family for the little girl and he held onto the secret for the rest of the day! He wanted to make sure I would always remember the moment when I found out about our new daughter.

It snowed the next day, Valentine's Day. We built a large snowman in the back yard (a real rarity in most of Texas) and took turns taking pictures of us in front of it. In the pictures, we held a large sign that read, "Happy Valentine's Day, Jae." When we later made a photo album to give to the foster family, those snow day pictures were on page one!

Reading the Child's Case File

If your family is selected for the child, the next step for you is to review the child's case file. The case file includes all information collected on the child since he or she was brought into foster care. Depending on how long the child has been in care, the file could be anywhere from a one-inch binder to several boxes of documents. Do not let a mountain of paperwork about your child frighten you off. The more information that has been collected and given to you the better it will be for you and your child in the long run.

Before the child's case file is given to you, it is "de-identified" to protect the child's confidentiality and those who may be connected with the child. Information that is generally withheld from the case file until you have read the file and formally accepted the child for adoptive placement includes the child's last name, social security number, names of the biological parents, and any current and previous addresses known. Most files will include information collected about the child, his/her parents, siblings (if any), grandparents and extended family members (depending on whether such information was available).

Information that may be included in the child's file;

- Investigation and assessment notes taken by state personnel

- Name, age, and nationality

- Birth certificate

- Physical description of the child

- Health status (In many states a medical examination is required no longer than thirty to ninety days before adoptive placement)

- Current immunization records

- Dental records (if applicable)

- A history chart of the child's physical development, including records of illnesses, abnormalities, development delays (if any) and health history

- Intellectual development, which includes any problems in intellectual development, any information known regarding the child's education, the child's enrollment and performance in school and if the child has special educational needs

- Cultural background, which includes child's day-to-day living, any special diets the child requires, behavior and discipline, information on all known abuse and neglect and the child's past and existing relationship with biological family members

- Child's personality

- Narratives of the child's adjustment to foster home(s), which includes a chronology of the child's placements, reasons for changes in placements and the child's reaction to those changes

- Child's legal status, which includes an affidavit of relinquishment signed by the child's biological parents (the parents gave up their rights to the child), or a signed and dated court order of parental rights termination (parents' right taken away by the state)

- Adoption readiness, which includes the child's thoughts about being adopted and his/her parent's inability to raise him/her

- Adoption assistance for the child

Information that may be included about the child's biological family (if available):

- Work histories

- Military service, if any

- Religious preferences and practices

- Education

- Medical histories and current health

- Physical description, including height, weight, and eye and hair color

- Personality

- Marriages, if any

- Divorces, if any

- Racial and ethnic backgrounds

- Criminal history

- Genetic history, including psychiatric, psychological and social histories and diagnoses

- If siblings not placed with this child, will there be arrangement for siblings to remain in contact with each other

- If deceased, the cause of death and the age at death

This "file" can be quite lengthy if the child has a history of medical issues and/ or was in the state's custody for a long time. Each piece of information the state has about the child is included. Much information about the child's family is included if it is available. In addition, each note taken by the social workers during visits with the biological parents, records of each doctor visit while the child was in state care, and assessments made by the foster family are included in the file. Even an infant's information can require several three-ring binders full of documentation.

After you review the child's case file, most states will not allow you to decide if you will accept the child right away. More than likely, you will be requested to wait 24 to 48 hours to make your decision. If you have just read a large binder (or several binders) on this child, you will need time to assimilate all of the information that you have read. Go back and re-read the file (or certain selections) before giving your final answer. Make a list of questions that you need answers to as you read the case file.

Note: If some information in the case file concerns you and makes you feel uneasy about accepting the child, talk to your caseworker about your concerns. Please also note that this information *may* be included. By no means will every file have all this information and all of the details. Many files have gaps and missing bits because the information is just unknown. Considering the history of some of these children, in some cases it is impossible to trace down everything.

Yes, We Will Take This Child!

If, after reading the child's file (perhaps more than once), you decide that you would like to proceed in adopting this child, call your worker and tell her/him of your decision. Your worker will then prepare to arrange a "presentation meeting" that will involve your family, your social worker, the social worker's supervisor, the child's worker, the child's worker's supervisor, and the foster parent(s), if any.

A presentation meeting brings together everyone involved with the child to discuss the plans of transitioning the child to the adoptive home. The social workers and supervisors of the state will tell you what they expect from you as the prospective adoptive parent(s). Here is a brief list of what the state may require:

- The child will be transitioned into your home at a slow pace and not necessarily on your time frame. Remember children need time to understand the process, to get to know you and prepare for the move and their good-byes.

- The child will have to be relatively comfortable with you before coming home with you to stay.

- You and the foster parents will work together in arranging pre-placement visits with the child.

- You must keep your social worker advised of all pre-placements visits arranged with the foster parents.

- Social worker will also be present at selected (or all) visits to observe.

- The photo album of your family may be requested at this time to help prepare the child.

You will also have your opportunity to ask any and all questions pertaining to your child. Generally, if the child is residing in a foster home, many of your questions may be directed to the child's foster parent(s). However, if you have more questions to ask your state agency, those questions are viable too. It is good for you to begin writing down questions that you will want to ask. Do not worry about asking too many questions. Everyone present will know that you are only interested in being prepared for your child.

Questions to ask if your child is an infant;

- How are/what are his/her eating habits?

- What type of formula is the child taking?

- How are his/her sleeping habits?

- Is he/she on a schedule?

- Is the child taking any medication?

- What size clothing does the child wear?

- Is it known if the child has been exposed to cocaine or other drugs? This kind of exposure can lead to very serious medical and physical problems with the child and requires careful consideration before proceeding.

- How is the child's general health? Many of these children have been exposed to situations that lead to health issues. Abuse, neglect, and drug/alcohol use can lead to many differing health problems that will have to be handled by the foster/adoptive parents.

- Is the child up to date on his/her shots?

- Has a Life Book been compiled? A Life Book is a combination scrapbook/life history of the child. Some states may call this by a different name, but it is a record of the child's life prior to adoptive placement. Typically foster parents compile a Life Book that the child may take with him to his new home.

Questions to ask if your child is a toddler;

- Is he/she potty trained?

- How are his/her eating habits? Likes and dislikes?

- What are his/her sleeping habits like?

- What are his/her fears?

- What does he/she like to play with?

- What are some of the child's interests?

- What size clothing and shoes does the child wear?

- Does the child like animals?

- Are there any known behavior issues?

- Has a Life Book been compiled?

Questions to ask if your child is of school age;

- How is the child doing in school?

- Are there issues and concerns with the child's education?

- How does the child seem to feel about himself/herself?

- How is he/she coping with the changes in his/her life?

- Is the child currently seeing a therapist or physician?

- Is he/she involved in extra-curricular activities?

If you think of additional questions during the actual presentation meeting, there will be plenty of time for you to get answers. And, you may be able to exchange phone numbers with the foster parents.

If your first pre-placement visit with your child is not scheduled with the foster parents during this meeting, it should be set to occur soon after the meeting.

6

Preparing for your Child's Arrival

What would have happened if Paul had allowed himself to be talked out of his journey to Damascus...

—Carl Jung, Swiss Psychologist, 1875–1961

As you prepare for your child's arrival, you will begin to see that your journey really is becoming a reality. Preparing for the arrival of your child is truly exciting; however, you may also experience stress or anxiety regarding upcoming events. And, you may feel pressured to get many tasks accomplished before your child arrives. You can relax, for now is the time when you get to actually enjoy the final preparations for bringing your child home.

Choosing Your Child's Name

If you are adopting an infant, you may have already chosen a new name for your child. In changing an infant's name, the immediate issues and concerns are few. However, if you are adopting a toddler or an older child, problems could result in changing the child's name. It is possible that changing a toddler or older child's name could result in confusion for your child.

Not only will the child have to deal with a change in environment and have to come to know a new family and new routines, but he or she will also get a new name. Changes such as these can result in a possible identity crisis at some point in the child's life. Also, the child may feel that he or she wants to hold onto the only "link" that he or she has to the past life with their birth family. Remember that even very young children long for this link to the past, even if they cannot remember their birth parents or family.

There are many reasons why adoptive parent(s) may feel that they should change a child's name. Perhaps the child is old enough to voice his or her opinion about wanting a name change. Alternatively, it may be that the adoptive parents just do not like the name the child was given at birth. Because no "right" or "wrong" answer exists when considering a name change for the child, the final decision belongs to the adoptive parent(s).

Note: I suggest that you discuss the child's possible name change with a child psychologist or a therapist who may have already been observing the child's behavior and moods. Input from a professional or a specialist in child development may help you in your decision to change your adoptive child's name.

Receiving Gifts from Well-Wishers

Whether you are adopting an infant or an older child, your friends may want to celebrate your happiness with a gift for the child. Consider registering at one or more of your favorite stores to help your friends in choosing a gift for your child. If you already know some of your child's favorite colors, toys, and likes, list these as gifts for people to purchase. In some cases, your child may need a new wardrobe because the old one is too old or non-existent. Make sure to get your child's sizes from his or her current caregivers. Also include on your list sizes that you think your child will be wearing in six to nine months. If you are not in need of gifts at the time your child arrives, ask for gift certificates to indoor playgrounds and gymnasiums, the local zoo, or family arcades.

Reminder: If your child is an infant, toddler, or preschooler, he or she may not come to you with a car or booster seat. You must possess a car or booster seat before driving home with children under age five.

Decorating Your Child's Room

You may have dreamed for months or years about decorating your child's room. Although, it may still be a month or so before your child is expected home, you will be eager to prepare the room.

Pre-placement visits with your child will help you to get to know your child. If your child is old enough to have preferences, then you can determine your child's likes and dislikes and incorporate these into the décor of the room. If your child is an infant or a toddler, you can be the one to choose the decorating scheme.

Enjoy your time of decorating. Enlist the help of others. Ask family members to donate used baby or children's furniture. Ask friends to help you paint furniture and walls (and, even the ceiling!). Plan a decorating "party" to get everyone involved in the arrival of your child. Each party invitee could even be asked to contribute an item or token that fits with the theme of the room.

Taking a Trip

You may feel that at this point in your journey you need to sit tight, remain close to home, and just await the arrival of your child. Remember, however, that your freedom and your personal schedule are about to be overturned! A weekend getaway may do you some good. Plan a night or two away to enjoy your life as it currently is. Read a good book on parenting. Eat ethnic foods that you've never before eaten. Go dancing. Enjoy yourself and reward yourself for being so diligent in your journey to adopt. And, most of all, relax and enjoy your getaway!

Beginning Pre-Placement Visits

Generally, pre-placement visits are arranged for the benefit of transitioning the child into his or her new environment. Depending on the age, development, and needs of your child, you may have to visit with him or her several times before time to bring the child home. Pre-placement visits are typically scheduled by you, the child (if applicable), the social worker, and/or foster parents. The younger the child is, the more frequently the pre-placement visits will occur.

If the child is a toddler or older, the photo album that you may have prepared months ago should be presented to the child before the first pre-placement visit.

The first visit typically is when the adoptive family meets the child in his or her current home. This gives the child a familiar setting in which to remain relaxed and secure. At this visit, you are welcome to bring a small gift to the child. It is usually recommended that no more than two or three family members of the adoptive family attend the first visit. During this first visit, there will be a caseworker who will monitor the entire visit.

The first visit may last one to three hours, depending on the child's age and needs. It is best if you prepare yourself not to expect a big welcome or even a hug from your child at the first meeting. In fact, you may not get any response from the child. Some children are very social with strangers. Others are shy or terrified of anyone whom they are not used to seeing or interacting with.

Two workers from the state observed our first visit. We all chatted nervously with the foster father for a short time before the foster mom brought Jae into the room. As the foster mom led Jae down the stairs, we all sat in silence. Jae didn't say anything when she was introduced to us. She merely stared and tried to hide behind her foster mother. She was obviously uncomfortable with so many strangers.

The adults began to make conversation among ourselves. We told the foster parents about our family and they talked about theirs. Within thirty minutes, we slowly began to relax just a bit. We had brought Jae an outfit to wear, a small doll, and an Easter basket (Easter had just passed). We thought the gifts would help break the ice with her.

I felt a little bit of a connection was made with Jae that night. The adults continued to talk together, while keeping our eyes locked on Jae as she played on the floor. It seemed as if she and our other daughter were making their own connection as well. They were playing with each other. Dirk later joined them in the middle of the floor and began talking and playing with Jae and her doll.

The photo album that we had previously sent to the foster family to prepare Jae for us was on the coffee table. As we talked, she picked the album up and began to look at our pictures. The foster mother asked her who each person was in the pictures. We heard Jae say, "Mommy, Daddy, and Morgan." The tears fell from my eyes. I was speechless. The foster family had done their part. They had used the album to prepare our child for us

As we prepared to leave, each of us asked Jae for a hug. We took three pictures of our visit. She didn't smile for any of them. It was okay, though. We were just happy to get photos of this first visit. When we left, we were on cloud nine!

Most of the time, there will be a second visit arranged not too long after the first visit. This visit can be set up in the child's home, or in a neutral setting such as a park, a restaurant, church where the child attends, or a playground. Depending on how the first visit went and how the child responded to you, it may be best if the current caregivers are present again. It is okay to accept the advice of the child's foster parents if they recommend that the child is not ready for a visit alone with your family. Try not to get caught up in hurrying into a time alone with your child without his or her current caregivers. The time alone with your child will come soon enough. It just has to be the right time for the child.

If the child is comfortable, the second visit may last longer than the first. There will probably be a caseworker on hand to monitor the second meeting. Depending on the state that you are adopting from and their procedures, the caseworker may stay for the whole visit or leave after seeing that the child is okay and comfortable. Any family members of the adoptive family who did not come to the first visit should be a part of this second visit.

Some children may require some time before they are comfortable in leaving their current home. If this is the case, many visits may take place in the foster home before you take the child to another location.

At some point, a visit should be scheduled for your own home. If the child is not comfortable being alone with your family just yet, the agreement may be made between you and the foster parents that they bring the child to your home. Perhaps you could have them over as a family for dinner or just to spend some time in your home. Show the child around, paying special attention to the room you have lovingly prepared for him or her. In most cases, the foster parents will do whatever is reasonably requested of them to help in transitioning the child into their new environment. Seeing you and the foster family interacting comfortably could help to soothe a nervous child.

Once the child is comfortable being alone with your family for several hours at a time, an overnight visit is usually scheduled. During the overnight visit, you should try to maintain the child's daily routine. There will be plenty of time, after bringing your child home for good, to gradually change the child's routine to mesh better with your family's schedule.

If the overnight visit goes well and the child is not experiencing any problems with being alone with your family, then you can then proceed in setting a placement date and begin making plans for the moving day.

We scheduled a date with the foster parents to bring Jae to our home for dinner. After dinner, the family talked with us a while, then they went home, leaving Jae with us for an overnight stay. We were afraid that Jae would get upset when the foster family left without her. But our fears proved to be groundless. She never seemed afraid or upset. After they left, we played with her for a couple of hours until it was time for her to go to bed. Watching her go to sleep in her own bed in our home was a dream come true.

7

Welcome Home

Journeys, like artists, are born and not made.
A thousand differing circumstances contribute to them...

Lawrence Durrell, British Author, 1912–1990

The day that you thought would never arrive is finally here! Today your child comes home. What an exciting time for your family! What a dramatic change in your family members' lives. This day marks the climax of all the emotions you have felt—emotions that are quite jumbled and unexplainable.

April 30 was the date to bring our precious daughter home. We had arranged a time in advance with her foster parents to pick up our daughter. We reflected on all that we had prepared for and endured from the first day of discussing adoption until this very day! Our treasure was now waiting for us just inside the door of her foster home.

As the door opened, she stood waiting for us with her belongings beside her. We loaded her things into our car in just minutes. She gave her foster family hugs and kisses and told them goodbye. Then, she happily walked out the door and hopped into our car. She never looked back and she never cried. She never questioned what was going on or showed any sign of fear. Not only were we in awe of the peace God had given her but, we were also grateful for how very well her foster family had prepared her for this important transition.

We laughed and talked all the way home. She was so very comfortable with us. At home, we unloaded her belongings and began to settle in for the night. We all felt, including our daughter's foster family, she had been specially picked for our family.

Adoptive Placement Agreement

The day that you bring your child home you will probably be required to sign an Adoptive Placement Agreement. By signing this, you are contracting with the state to carry out the adoptive parents' roles and responsibilities for the child until the adoption is finalized. Some aspects of this agreement may be as follows:

- Adoptive parent(s) sign with the understanding of a supervisory period of several months to a year (depending on the state) before the adoption can be legally finalized.

- During the supervisory period, and pending finalization of the adoption, the adoptive parents are expected to assume full financial responsibility for the child.

- As the child is still in the legal custody of state, you must obtain authorization before traveling out-of-state with the child.

- You must obtain authorization for any non-emergency medical care before it is provided.

The agreement will generally list the roles and responsibilities of the state with the adoptive parent(s) as well. Some of the state worker's responsibilities may include, but may not be limited to:

- Discuss and determine the need for adoption assistance and post adoption services.

- Assist the adoptive parents with any services that the child may need.

- Assist and arrange for the adoptive parents to finalize the adoption after the supervisory period ends.

- Ensure that the adoptive family has received the child's social security card and new birth certificate.

In some cases, you may be given these documents again during the signing of the placement agreement:

- A copy of the child's Health, Social, Educational and Genetic History report (HSEGH)

- A copy of the state's Child Discipline Policy

- A signed, medical consent form for the child

- Information about your state's Adoption Assistance Program

Signing our Placement Agreement April 30 was the next best thing to consummation of our adoption. Actually signing the paperwork made it more official for us. We could hardly wait for the caseworker to explain all the paperwork and leave. We were anxiously waiting to start our new life with our daughter. (The caseworker probably sensed our eagerness!) After signing the papers, we asked our caseworker to take a picture of our new family. Though just a snapshot, it was our first family picture!

Observation Period with Your Child

Being in a new environment and with new people can be frightening and uncomfortable for anyone, especially for a child. If you have an infant, the changes for him/her may not be drastic enough for you to see. However, for a toddler or an older child, this adjustment may be very visible.

If your child is old enough to understand the purpose of his new home and surroundings, it is advisable to talk with him/her about their new environment and how they may be feeling. Children are resilient. They really can bounce back to "normal" after major changes. However, time is the key in allowing children to get used to their surroundings and feel comfortable with all aspects of their new lives.

With an older child, it may be good to let her roam the house (within reason) to get familiar with her new environment. It is also important that your child begin to learn the rules and boundaries that have been set in place. After bringing your child home, you may think that for the first few weeks your child can or should have several freedoms in the home or do whatever he or she wants. And, if you are a new parent, you may believe that the "house rules" can be established at a later time when your child is more relaxed with your family. Waiting until later to put the house rules into place may not be a good idea.

Parents always want to help their child as much as possible in transitioning into his new environment. However, children, whether adopted or not, need established boundaries and rules as soon as they realize who the rule makers are. As the parent or parents, you are the rule maker(s) and your child sees you as such. So, it is important to set boundaries in place right away. This will give your child a structured environment from the get-go and provide the security and consistency that every child needs.

Though this is not a complete list, here are a few things that you may want to closely observe the first few days your child is in his or her new home:

- Sleeping and eating habits appropriate to age

- Sensory skills appropriate to age

- Motor skills appropriate to age

- Social skills for child's age

- Physical abilities for child's age

- Language skills for child's age

- Level of awareness of new environment

The child's previous caregiver may have already shared with you some of these observations concerning your child, but it is always good for you to observe and study these for yourself. Make note of any significant changes from prior behavior.

The first night that our daughter was officially home, we could not take our eyes off of her. We watched her every move. She played with a favorite toy that she could not put down for quite some time. We believed that night that she was truly the happiest kid in the world. Later, she began to tour her new environment. We allowed her to do so, but constantly followed her to each room.

Although Jae seemed happy and laughed aloud with us often, she didn't talk very much. I remember three things that she said often and clear: "Thank you," "I need to go potty," and "I wanna' wash my hands." We thought that these statements from her were just precious! Her social and language skills were lacking somewhat, however, we felt that most of her shyness was from her lack of being able to communicate effectively with others.

Our daughter's eating habits were wonderful right from the start. We didn't have to wait for her to develop a good appetite for food. At times, she was almost eating more than our 11-year-old daughter. There was not much that she didn't like to eat. She had a cute way of finishing everything on her plate, then pushing her plate away from her and saying, "Done."

Her sleeping habits were great as well. She has slept in her own bed since the first night she arrived at our home. She has slept the entire night through except for a couple of nights. Her bedroom is upstairs and our master bedroom is downstairs. We had agreed that we would sleep in a spare room upstairs until we knew that our new daughter was safe, comfortable, and sleeping all night. Watching her peacefully sleeping almost every hour throughout the night, we didn't get a lot of sleep ourselves, but, after seeing how she did the first night, we knew she would be okay sleeping alone.

Bonding with Your Child

What an important time this will be for you and your child during these first few days and weeks. There is still so much to learn about each other. For now, you are still practically strangers to one another. However, the early days of bonding with your child are crucial.

Bonding with a newborn may not be as difficult as with a toddler or an older child. With a toddler or older child, there is a previous life that they have left behind, one that may cause them to fear change, or it could be one that they wish to return to. Whatever situation your toddler or older child came from, the former life is a loss to them. This former life was what they had and all they knew.

The following are some things that you can do to help during this bonding period with your child:

• Sing, laugh, read, play, and talk

- Hold, hug, and kiss (depending on his age and if your child will allow this)

- Establish a routine in your child's schedule and be consistent

- Continue to have patience

- Say "I love you" often

- Older children may want to help with household chores as this can make them feel needed

Although this is not a complete list of what you can do to help you and your child bond with each other, it definitely is a start. Even with doing some or many of the things listed above, you must still allow your child time to bond with you especially if he is a toddler or older child.

We felt that our daughter and our family had made a special connection with each other even before she came home. She was always happy to see us after the first pre-placement visit we had with her. To this day she has never asked about her past life. We took pictures of her previous caregivers and have shown them to her often. She smiles and is happy to see their picture, but has never asked where they are or if she can go back.

The bonding relationship that our daughter and our family share has only grown stronger since her arrival into our home. She knows that she is loved dearly by us all. It is such a great feeling when she says, "I love you" to one of us without us initially saying it to her first. She smiles often and tells us, "I'm happy." We feel that she is truly a blessing. We also know that this kind of bonding is not always the case when adopting a toddler or an older child.

Post-Placement Visits from the Adoption Worker

In most cases, during the placement period, you will see a placement worker each month. Most states require face-to-face contacts with the adoptive parent(s) on a regular basis for a period of time. These monthly meetings are normally required to be in your home and with the child present. In most states, all family members who live in the home are also required to be present. The worker's purpose for meeting with you on a monthly basis is to assess the child and your family's adjustment and attachment with each other. If you are in need of post-adoption assistance, the worker will assist you in finding the service(s) you may need.

We had an awesome placement worker. We actually looked forward to our monthly visits with her and didn't want to see them end. Since the day our family was accepted by the state as an adoptive home, we were very fortunate in getting and working with a professional placement worker. During each visit to our house, she asked questions and always took notes. If there was anything that we needed, we knew that we could depend on her to get the answer we needed.

After the fourth month's visit, our little daughter even looked forward to the placement worker's visits to our home. On the last two visits, our daughter greeted her with big hugs and huge smiles. We felt that our little one knew that our worker was visiting to check on just her!

Limit Visitors for a While

Everyone you are close to will want to rush over and meet your newest addition. It may be best to talk to family members and friends before bringing your child home. Help them to understand the importance of your time alone with your child the first few days. It will be hard for loved ones to stay away, but with proper explanation ahead of time you could possibly eliminate any hurt feelings.

Your child's age will have a major affect on when you allow visitors to come over. While a newborn may not even know the difference as long as the visitors are not unruly, an older child may need time to adjust to the new environment as well as with the new immediate family members. Other people and other distractions could delay or disrupt the initial bonding process.

We prepared our family and friends ahead of time before bringing our child home. Everyone was very thoughtful and understanding of the time that we needed to have alone with our daughter. We received many phone calls the first day she was home, but no one harassed us about coming over to see her. On her fifth day with us, we took her to visit a few family members. We gradually introduced more family and friends to her. We thought that it would be best not to throw her into a crowd of strangers too quickly.

Begin Preparing a Lifebook

A lifebook can be one of the best things that you can have for your adoptive child. A lifebook is similar to a scrapbook; however, a lifebook is a record of your child's life, starting from birth to the present time. The child's history is told in many more words than you would put into a scrapbook of just photos.

A lifebook may include some of the following and more:

- Birth certificate

- Health problems notated at birth

- Birth photos, if available

- Photos of birth parents, if available

- More photos of the adoptee

- Copies of letters or other important documents

- Discussion of birth mother and birth father if available

- Discussion of why child was adopted

A lifebook validates the child's history. It can help your adoptive child in more ways than you can imagine. A lifebook will not be important to an infant or toddler right away. However, as the child gets older and begins to ask questions, you will be able to present this wonderful gift of history. This compilation of events and memories is something your child will treasure forever. It can also be a book that a child can go back to as often as they like and look at throughout their life.

Within the first couple of weeks of bringing Jae home, I started a scrapbook for her. She looks at it often with big smiles. The sad part of our daughter's book is that it will not contain many baby pictures of her. Not having more baby pictures of her weighed heavily on my mind. I have begun to wonder how much the lack of baby pictures may affect our daughter when she is older and does not have these early pictures to look at.

Eventually, I called the hospital where our daughter was born with hopes of them having her pictures on file. The operator transferred me to the "photo" people. A sweet woman listened to what I was wanting and then said that she would not be able to help me get the pictures that were taken years ago. She also mentioned that there was another photo company before her company and that this company was no longer in business.

Through another source, however, I got in touch with the owner of the previous photography company and explained my story and request to him. He mentioned that the photos taken from that far back had already been destroyed but he would check and call me back. Within forty-five minutes, he called me back to say that he was right, the photos for this particular year had been destroyed, but, he added, "For some reason your child's photos are still here and where would you like me to send them?"

Wow! I was blown away! During his call back, we talked for a little while. Near the end of the conversation, he said to me, "Thanks for adopting her." I thought it was a strange comment. Then he said, "I was adopted, too, at the age of sixteen, and I was saved."

Another wow! What seemed like a dead end, turned out to be another amazing story that we will share with Jae one day. Was this man another of the "angels" who had been looking out for us during this journey?

Write your Announcement

While there are several ways to make the announcement of your new addition known to others, writing an announcement card or letter about your new little one to family and friends will be exciting for you and for them. You can write as little or as much as you wish to share with others. Most people who you are close to will not mind the details you want to share.

We waited about a month after bringing home our daughter before we sent out an announcement letter to our family and friends. We also included a picture of her in each announcement. Although many family and friends had yet to meet her, they got to see a picture of her.

In our announcement, we shared details of the first month of her time at home with us and we also shared the kind of child she was. We included enough in the announcement letter to catch everyone up on what was taking place with our newest addition. We had many people to tell us that they enjoyed the details of the letter.

A new beginning has truly begun for you and for your child. Your child is safe at home now and your family feels complete. The many changes that you already feel that have taken place in your family are countless. Treasure this special time now and forever.

8

Financial Matters

"Good company in a journey makes the way seem shorter."

Izaak Walton, British Writer, 1593–1683

Adoption assistance, also known as adoption subsidies, are provided by state and federal governments to ensure that adoptive parents can meet the financial responsibilities of children with special needs.

Children with special needs are generally more difficult to place for adoption due to extenuating circumstances, such as their age; membership in a minority or sibling group; and/or mental, emotional, or physical difficulties.

If you are considering adopting a child with special needs, you should learn about the subsidy policy in your state. Each state has its own definition of "special needs." Each state also sets its own subsidy payment ceiling and process for negotiating subsidy amounts. See Appendix D for a subsidy profile for each state. These rates/payments can change with the states and sometimes with federal regulations.

The Title IV-E Adoption Assistance Program

The Title IV-E Adoption Assistance Program is a state funded program that is required of all states. The intent of the program is to reduce the barriers to adoption of children with special needs. The children must meet certain criteria to qualify for this program.

Under section 473(c) of the Act, the following are necessary:

- The state has determined that the child cannot or should not be returned to his parents.

- The state has determined that the child's age; ethnic background; membership in a minority group or sibling group; or physical, mental, or emotional challenges are such that it is reasonable to conclude that such child cannot be placed for adoption without adoption assistance.

- The state has determined that a reasonable, but unsuccessful, effort has been made to place with an appropriate adoptive family without providing adoption assistance.

Several benefits are available through adoption assistance program such as:

- Financial Assistance

- Medicaid Coverage

- Reimbursement for Non-recurring Adoption Expenses

Financial assistance pays up to the amount the state would have paid during the same period if the child had remained in foster care. Some states begin financial assistance payments as soon as the child is placed with a family. Other states, however, may not begin payments until the child's adoption is finalized.

Medicaid coverage automatically begins for children who are eligible for the federal adoption assistance programs. Medicaid coverage may also be available through state adoption assistance programs. Medicaid benefits transfer from state-to-state if your family moves.

Some states reimburse non-recurring adoption expenses to the adoptive parents of special needs children. The adoptive parents may receive reimbursement for these non-recurring adoption expenses. Expenses may include adoption fees, court costs, attorney fees, transportation expenses, and other expenses related to the legal adoption of a child with special needs.

State Adoption Subsidy

Non-Title IV-E children are state funded. If your child does not qualify for the Title IV-E program, he/she may be eligible for another subsidy program funded by the state. It may vary from state to state, but more often than not, your child will have the same benefits as if he/she had qualified under the Title IV-E program.

The Adoption Policy Resource Center (http://www.fpsol.com/adoption/) recommends that prospective adoptive parents make a checklist of questions to discuss with their agency in regards to adoption assistance programs.

Your checklist should include the following questions:

• Have I had an extensive discussion with agency adoption professionals about the present and future needs of my child and about the information and services that will be required to meet his/her needs?

• Have I had extensive discussion about my family's resources concerning the availability of information, financial resources, and support services that will enable our family to successfully incorporate this child into a new family?

• Have I been encouraged to view adoption assistance programs and post-adoption services as essential parts of a post-adoption support plan for a child who either has, or is at risk to develop, some special needs?

• Have I (or has the agency) explored eligibility for the Federal Social Security Income (SSI) program?

• Do I understand that, according to federal law, agencies cannot refuse to act on an application for the Title IV-E adoption assistance or reimbursement of non-recurring adoption expenses? The agency must respond in writing to each application.

- Do I understand that my child's eligibility for Title IV-E adoption assistance does not depend on my family's income or financial resources, but only on my child's situation?

- Do I understand the amount of adoption assistance is determined by an individual, written agreement with the agency?

- Do I understand that if an agreement for adoption assistance or reimbursement for non-recurring expenses is not signed prior to the finalization of the adoption, the subsidy can only be awarded by appeal through administrative fair hearing?

These are only some of the questions that the prospective adoptive parent(s)may want to ask. Others may not be listed here.

Negotiating Adoption Subsidy Agreements

The Adoption Subsidy Agreement must be written and is a legal document that is binding on all parties, which would include the prospective adoptive parents, the state or local adoption agency, and any other relevant agencies. Negotiating the subsidy generally takes place before the child is placed in your home, though it is not unheard of for the negotiations to come after placement. In all cases, you must make sure that you have negotiated and signed the subsidy agreement *before* the final adoption hearing.

Many things will be written into the agreement, such as the following:

- The kind of assistance determined for your child, which would be one of the following: Title IV-E and/or Medicaid, State Adoption Financial Assistance and/or Medicaid, State Medical Assistance, or Non-Recurring Adoption Expenses reimbursement.

- The responsibilities of the prospective adoptive parents to the agency which would include, but are not limited to, the following: notify agency of address changes or changes in the child's placement, payee changes, child's living arrangement or income changes, petition to adopt is filed and when adoption is consummated by the court.

- The amount of funds that will be paid to the adoptive parents each month.

- The date the adoption assistance begins. The child will have to be living in your home before assistance begins.

- The date adoption assistance will end. This generally occurs when the child reaches age 18–21, on the parent's request, on the removal or death of the child, or on termination of the parent's legal responsibility for the child, or when the parents no longer support the child.

Fair Hearings and Adoption Assistance Appeals

A fair hearing or an adoption assistance appeal is a process for settling differences between adoptive parents and the public agency that administers the program. If the adoptive parents feel that they have been wrongly denied benefits on behalf of an adoptive child, they have the right to a fair hearing.

The Child Welfare Policy Manual under section 8.4G (Fair Hearings) lists six allegations that constitute grounds for a fair hearing:

1. Relevant facts regarding the child were known by the state agency or child-placing agency and not presented to the adoptive parents before finalization of the adoption.

2. Denial of assistance based on a means test of the adoptive family.

3. The adoptive family disagrees with the determination by the state that a child is ineligible for adoption assistance.

4. Failure by the state agency to advise potential adoptive parents about the availability of adoption assistance for children in the state foster care system.

5. Decrease in the amount of the adoption assistance without the concurrence of the adoptive parents.

6. Denial of a request for a change in payment level due to a change in the adoptive parents circumstances.

In cases where the final fair hearing is favorable to the adoptive parents, the state agency can reverse the earlier decision to deny benefits under Title IV-E.

Adoption Tax Credit

As of 2004, and increasing thereafter, if your family earns less than $155,860 per year, you may qualify for an adoption tax credit of up to $10,390 for qualifying expenses paid to adopt an eligible child. Higher incomes can also be eligible for tax credit(s) at a reduced rate. Qualifying adoption expenses include court costs, attorney fees, traveling expenses, and other expenses related to the legal adoption of an eligible child. If you are adopting a special needs child, you can receive the maximum credit, even if you do not have any qualifying expenses. Some states also offer tax credits for adoptive families

Check with a tax professional or the IRS for compete details of how the adoption tax credit will benefit you.

9

Finalizing Your Adoption

"Press forward. Do not stop, do not linger in your journey,
but strive for the mark set before you."

George Whitefield, 1714–1770, Founder of the Methodist Church

Legally finalizing your child's adoption is a big deal, although the finalization hearing is just a formality. The finalization of an adoption is when the child becomes legally your child. It involves demonstrating to a judge that the child is legally free for adoption and that you have had enough experience with the child that you can honestly promise to raise her as your own. The court hearing takes approximately 15 to 20 minutes.

Finding an Adoption Attorney

More than likely, you will need an adoption attorney to help finalize the adoption. There are several ways to go about finding one. You can look in the yellow pages or even locate one through the Internet. However, it may be best to ask others who have adopted a child whom they used. Most adoptive parents who have had a good experience will be happy to tell you who they hired. Before hiring an attorney, there are certain questions you should ask, such as:

- What is the average cost of the adoptions you have handled?

- How do you bill?

- Do you require a retainer fee in advance?

- What is your experience and knowledge?

- How long have you worked in adoption?

- How many adoptions do you handle a year?

- What is your general philosophy about adoption?

- Why did you get involved in adoption?

- Do you have any references?

Make sure that you are comfortable with the attorney's answers to these questions. In the end, the decision is yours. Do not put off hiring an attorney once you get your child. Make this a priority on your list to find an attorney as soon as possible.

We never looked through the yellow pages or the Internet to find our attorney. We just asked several parents in our support group whom they had used to finalize their adoption. Because of the good experiences they had with their attorneys, there was no problem for them to make recommendations. This also made us feel more secure and comfortable about the attorney. Knowing also what questions to ask an attorney made the interview a lot easier for us. We called two attorneys. Both of their practices related solely to adoptions. Therefore, our choice was made rather quickly.

Role of an Adoption Attorney

The adoption attorney plays a big part in making sure that your adoption is finalized. Your attorney helps you understand everything that has to take place before the finalization hearing. He will make sure that all documents are filed with the court in a timely manner. He will also convince the judge that you are qualified in adopting your child and that there is no reason why you should not be allowed to adopt.

In most cases, the attorney warns you ahead of time what will happen during the finalization hearing. The attorney will do most of the talking. He will tell you the questions that he will ask and that you will have to answer.

Our attorney was wonderful! Once we hired him, he did all the leg work for us to get us where we needed to be on court day. He told us from the start what documents he would need to file the petition with the court on our behalf. He truly made the process seem so simple.

Adoption Petition

By filing an adoption petition, you are formally requesting legal permission to adopt your child. To file a petition, you will need the following information and documentation:

- Your name, age, and address

- The child's birth certificate

- A written statement that the adoption is in the child's best interest

- The date on which you received custody of the child

- A statement showing the birth parents' right are terminated

Filing the adoption petition with the court is generally something that your attorney will handle with your assistance.

Court Appearance Day

The day you go to court will be a very special day for your family. The end of your adoption journey is almost in sight. You will be extremely nervous before you even get to the court building. You will want to arrive a little earlier than your hearing start time. You will also want to dress up for this occasion, because you are typically allowed to take pictures to remember this day.

In most cases, you are encouraged to invite extended family members and friends to attend the hearing with you. Try to plan for some kind of celebration for your child afterwards.

Our finalization hearing was set for November 20, National Adoption Day. Our time to appear in front of the judge was 8:30 a.m. We arrived at the court at approximately 8 a.m. We began to sense the excitement of the experience before we even got inside our courtroom.

When we walked through the door of the court building, we were greeted by friendly volunteers. On the inside, the corridors and halls were decorated in a childlike setting with lots of balloons and clowns everywhere. Outside each court-room door that each family would enter, there were balloons to greet the families. It was an awesome feeling knowing that so much time and effort had been put into this day for not only our child but many others as well.

There was a news crew interviewing different families. There was a professional photographer onsite photographing each family. After our family picture was taken, we were given a CD of the pictures so we could get them developed ourselves.

This was the end! It was a very exciting, yet also a nerve-racking time for all of us. We knew that it would all be over by 9 a.m., but the nervous, jittery feelings of excitement and anticipation were just overwhelming. We did invite a few family members to join us.

At 8:25 a.m. our attorney led us into our courtroom where we would appear in front of the judge.

Questions That You Will Be Asked

As mentioned earlier, your attorney may have met with you earlier to prep you on the types of questions that he will ask you at the hearing. Do not be too concerned about surprise questions. Usually, there aren't any. First you will be sworn in under oath that you are being truthful with your answers. You will be asked to state your full name and spell it. You will also have to give your address. Here is a list of some questions that you will be asked:

- The date your child was placed in your home

- The date of your marriage

- The date of your child's birth

- If you understand that your child will have all legal rights as if she was born to you and will inherit from you equally

- If you understand that you are financially responsible for your child if the marriage ends in divorce or if one parent dies

In most cases, only one parent has to answer these questions. If this is the case, the other parent will only be asked if he or she agrees with the spouse's testimony.

I was happy to let my husband be the brave one to endure all of the questions during our hearing. I warned him ahead of time that he would be the one. As nervous as I was, I could only imagine forgetting our marriage date or the city in which we lived.

Our attorney did prepare us ahead of time with the questions he would ask us. Actually, he made it even easier than what we had heard from other adoptive parents' court experiences. Our attorney's questions required only answers of "yes" or "no." The entire hearing lasted for about twelve minutes.

We were allowed to take pictures with the judge and with our extended family members in the courtroom. We received our adoption decree before leaving the court. It was truly a joyous day for us. However, it was also a relief that this was the end of our "journey" and our daughter was legally ours forever.

10

Connecting with a Support Group

"The kindness and affection from the public have carried me through some of the most difficult periods, and always your love and affection have eased the journey."

Diana, 1961–1997, Princess of Wales

Not only does adopting a child bring rewards to a family, but it can also bring challenges. Adoptive parents often need to talk with other adoptive parents who understand the unique challenges in raising an adoptive child. Your family and friends, though supportive, may not fully understand your concerns regarding adoption. The right support group can be a wonderful experience for adoptive parents and children.

Support groups are often formed by foster and adoptive parents who desire to be of assistance to other parents or prospective parents in whatever way is necessary to meet their needs and concerns with their children. The more experienced members will be able to answer many of the questions you may still have regarding adoption. You may also meet other prospective parents, like you, who wonder about some of the same things that concern you. There are numerous ways that a support group can help your family.

My husband and I were fortunate in getting involved in a wonderful support group. Before we finished our PRIDE classes, a local support group contacted us. After speaking to one of the adoptive parents from the group, we were very interested in attending one of their meetings. Becoming members of a support group proved to be very beneficial to us. It gave us more comfort in knowing that we could share our problems and concerns with a group of people who could relate to what we were experiencing at different points in our journey.

Locating a Support Group

Locating a group to meet your needs can be a lot of work. There are many groups that are active in every state. The North American Council on Adoptable Children (NACAC) provides a list of parent support groups organized by state. And, your caseworker may be able to lead you to a group in your area. See Appendix B for a list of support groups you might be interested in speaking with.

Benefits of a Support Group

Journeying through the world of adoption can be exciting and at the same time, frightening, for many prospective parents. Contacting your local adoption support group and linking up with people who have already adopted can definitely be rewarding. Support groups can offer many things to foster and adoptive parents, including the following:

- **Providing encouragement and hope.** Meeting people who have already traveled the path you are considering can help you to understand that you are not alone. No matter what question or problem you may have, someone has probably experienced it before. Getting first-hand advice may not provide an immediate solution, but it can be comforting to know that your issues aren't unique.

- **Sharing knowledge.** The combined experience of a group, especially a large one, can be extensive. The type of person who leads a support group is the type who truly desires to help others. This person will gladly offer their advice to those new to fostering/adopting.

- **Providing education.** Some parents are only interested in fostering children, while others want to continue to foster children after they have adopted one or more. Most states require some sort of continuing education for foster parents. The support groups may offer those parents a chance to receive their continuing education credits at a reduced cost or for free. Even parents not required to participate in continuing education can benefit from the training these classes offer.

- **Providing peace of mind.** Sometimes just sharing the problems of raising a child (adoptive or not) can be a blessing. A sympathetic ear and a shoulder to cry on can be very therapeutic for the new parents.

- **Helping find the right child.** Because many of the members of the support group may be fostering children, they may be able to lead prospective adoptive parents to children they know of or who they are caring for at the time. My husband and I know of at least two occasions where one member of our support group adopted a child they met while the child was being fostered by another member of the same support group!

- **Offering social gatherings.** Support groups can become like a second family. Many members become fast friends outside of the "walls" of the group. Oftentimes, the group may offer holiday parties and events for special occasions. The group may also schedule trips to a circus, fair, amusement park, or other event, sometimes offering reduced rates or free admission to foster/adoptive families.

There were a few times where my husband and I needed encouragement during our journey. Before ever starting our PRIDE classes, we did a lot of research on the Internet. With the abundance of information that can be found on the Internet regarding adoption, it can still leave the prospective parents totally confused on a lot of the questions and concerns they may have. As part of a support group, we were able to meet "real" adoptive parents who shared the ups and downs they experienced during their journeys. Some stories we heard would definitely give any prospective parents hope that adoption could happen for them as well.

We heard many stories at our group. There were more positive stories than negative ones. The negative stories would often be from prospective parents who were feeling discouraged that they were still waiting for their child. Mostly, parents shared why they decided to adopt and how much happiness adoption or fostering had brought to their families. Others shared how long it took them to adopt and how it was all worth it. For me, it was great to talk with an adoptive parent who had "made it" and who could offer me suggestions or answers to the questions I had.

My husband and I felt that the topics that were discussed in our support group were very helpful. Our group meets twice a month. At each meeting, there is always something that is educational and also something that we do not know about as adoptive parents.

Support groups can also be valuable for an adoptive child. Children who are adopted may feel that they are different and that there's no one else in the world like them. Being part of a group can oftentimes alleviate the concerns an adoptive child has in feeling alone. In the right group, the child can:

- Meet other children who are adopted

- See other families that are similar to their own

- Become friends with other adoptive children

- Communicate easier with other adoptive children

- Share their feelings as an adoptive child

There are many adoption support groups formed nationally. The task is to find the right group that fits your family and your family's needs.

JOURNEY'S END

We all make our own plans in life, or so we think. We make plans about marriage and the kind of person we want to marry. We decide if we want to have children and how many. Sometimes we go so far as to plan *when* we will marry and *when* we will have children. And, it takes a while for us to realize that our plans rarely happen as we wish.

My lifelong dream of having two children was fulfilled, but not exactly as I had planned it. The joy that we have experienced in bringing Jaelyn into our family has been wonderful. There have been many new experiences that we never could have planned. These experiences will continue to affect our lives forever.

Though I consider my family's adoption experience to be a successful and happy journey, not all adoptive parents can say the same. Every adoption journey is different. Many of the children in foster care have been abused or neglected and the chances of that "happily ever after" ending are slim. However, it's not impossible either.

Anyone seeking to adopt, whether through their state's foster care system or by other means, should understand that these children often have real issues that do not end just because the children get adopted into loving and caring homes.

My family has completed a long journey where each step along the way was a step of faith and determination. Now we begin a new journey, a new life, and a new family. We wish success to you as you begin your own journey, one step at a time.

Your journey never ends. Life has a way of changing things in incredible ways.

Alexander Volkov, Russian novelist, 1891–1977

Appendix A

State Child Welfare Agencies and Web Pages

Every state and the District of Columbia has a website dedicated to helping families adopt children from the foster care system. These websites help prospective adoptive or foster families to contact the agency workers they need to reach to get started. They introduce the families to the concepts involved and sometimes allow families to see actual pictures of the children waiting to be adopted.

Alabama Department of Human Resources
http://www.dhr.state.al.us/
Adoption and Foster Care Information:
http://www.dhr.state.al.us/page.asp?pageid=306
State Adoption Exchange/Photolisting Service:
http://www.adoptuskids.org/states/al
Alaska Department of Health and Social Services
http://www.hss.state.ak.us/
Adoption and Foster Care Information:
http://www.hss.state.ak.us/ocs/
State Adoption Exchange/Photolisting Service:
http://www.nwae.org
Please contact: (907) 465-3631

Arizona Department of Economic Security
http://www.de.state.az.us
Adoption and Foster Care Information:
http://www.de.state.az.us/dcyf/adoption
State Adoption Exchange/Photolisting Service:
http://www.de.state.az.us/dcyf/adoption/meet.asp

Arkansas Department of Human Services
http://www.state.ar.us/dhs/
Adoption and Foster Care Information:
http://www.state.ar.us/dhs/adoption/adoption.html
http://www.state.ar.us/dhs/chilnfam/
State Adoption Exchange/Photolisting Service:
http://www.state.ar.us/dhs/adoption/adoption.html

California Department of Social Services
http://www.dss.cahwnet.gov
Adoption and Foster Care Information:
http://www.childsworld.ca.gov/CFSDAdopti_309.htm
http://www.childsworld.ca.gov/FosterCare_310.htm
State Adoption Exchange/Photolisting Service:
http://www.CAKidsConnection.com

Colorado Department of Human Services
http://www.cdhs.state.co.us/
Adoption and Foster Care Information:
http://www.cdhs.state.co.us/cyf/cwelfare/cwweb.html
State Adoption Exchange/Photolisting Service:
http://www.adoptex.org
http://www.changealifeforever.org/children.asp
Adoption and Foster Care Information:
http://www.state.ct.us/dcf/foster.htm
State Adoption Exchange/Photolisting Service:
http://www.adoptuskids.org/states/ct

Delaware Department of Services for Children, Youth and Their Families
http://www.state.de.us/kids/
Adoption and Foster Care Information:
http://www.state.de.us/kids/adoption.htm
http://www.state.de.us/kids/fostercare.htm
State Adoption Exchange/Photolisting Service:
http://www.adopt.org/
District of Columbia Child and Family Services Agency
Adoption and Foster Care Information: contact (202)727-4550

Florida Department of Children and Families
http://www.state.fl.us/cf_web
Adoption and Foster Care Information:
http://www.myflorida.com/cf_web/myflorida2/healthhuman/adoption/search/
index.shtml
http://www.dcf.state.fl.us/fostercare/
State Adoption Exchange/Photolisting Service:
http://www.myflorida.com/cf_web/myflorida2/healthhuman/adoption/search/
index.shtml

Georgia Department of Human Resources
http://www.dhr.state.ga.us/
Adoption and Foster Care Information:
http://www.adoptions.dhr.state.ga.us/
State Adoption Exchange/Photolisting Service:
http://www.myturnnow.com/

Hawaii Department of Human Services
http://www.state.hi.us/dhs/index.html
Adoption and Foster Care Information:
http://www.state.hi.us/dhs/index.html
State Adoption Exchange/Photolisting Service:
Please contact: (808) 586-5698

Idaho Department of Health and Welfare
http://www.state.id.us/health_safety/
Division of Family and Community Services
http://www.healthandwelfare.idaho.gov/portal/alias_Rainbow/lang_en-US/
tabID_3326/DesktopDefault.aspx
Adoption Exchange/Photolisting Service:
http://www.nwae.org
http://www.idahowednesdaychild.org

Illinois Department of Children and Family Services
http://www.state.il.us/dcfs/
Adoption and Foster Care Information:
http://www.state.il.us/dcfs/

State Adoption Exchange/Photolisting Service:
http://www.adoptinfo-il.org

Indiana Family and Social Services Administration
http://www.state.in.us/fssa/
Adoption and Foster Care Information:
http://www.state.in.us/fssa/adoption/process.html
State Adoption Exchange/Photolisting Service:
http://www.state.in.us/fssa/adoption/

Iowa Department of Human Services
http://www.dhs.state.ia.us/
Adoption and Foster Care Information:
http://www.dhs.state.ia.us/ACFS/ACFS.asp
State Adoption Exchange/Photolisting Service:
http://www.iakids.org

Kansas Department of Social and Rehabilitation Services
http://www.srskansas.org
Adoption and Foster Care Information:
http://www.srskansas.org/services/adoption.htm
http://www.srskansas.org/services/fostercare.htm
State Adoption Exchange/Photolisting Service:
http://www.cominghomekansas.org

Kentucky Cabinet for Families and Children
http://cfc.state.ky.us/
Adoption and Foster Care Information:
http://cfc.state.ky.us/help/adoption.asp
State Adoption Exchange/Photolisting Service:
http://cfc.state.ky.us/cbs-snap/search.asp

Louisiana Department of Social Services
http://www.dss.state.la.us/
Adoption and Foster Care Information:
http://www.dss.state.la.us/departments/ocs/Adoption_Services.html
http://www.dss.state.la.us/departments/ocs/Foster_Parents.html
State Adoption Exchange/Photolisting Service:

http://www.adoptuskids.org/states/la/

Maine Department of Health and Human Services
http://www.maine.gov/dhhs/bcfs/index.htm
State Adoption Exchange/Photolisting Service:
http://www.adoptudkids.org/states/me

Maryland Department of Human Resources
http://www.dhr.state.md.us/
Adoption and Foster Care Information:
http://www.dhr.state.md.us/ssa/adopt.htm
http://www.dhr.state.md.us/ssa/foster/index.htm
State Adoption Exchange/Photolisting Service:
http://www.adoptuskids.org/states/md/

Massachusetts Department of Social Services
http://www.mass.gov/dss
Adoption and Foster Care Information:
http://www.mass.gov/portal/index.jsp?pageID=eohhs2subtopic&L=4&sid=
Eeohhs2&L0=Home&L1=Consumer&L2=Family+Services&L3=Adoption
http://www.mass.gov/portal/index.jsp?pageID=eohhs2topic&L=4&L0=Home
&L1=Consumer&L2=Family+Services&L3=Foster+Care&sid=Eeohhs2
State Adoption Exchange/Photolisting Service:
http://www.adoptuskids.org/states/ma/browse.html

Michigan Family Independence Agency
http://www.michigan.gov/fia
Adoption and Foster Care Information:
http://www.michigan.gov/fia/1,1607,7-124-5452_7116—,00.html
http://www.michigan.gov/fia/1,1607,7-124-5452_7117—,00.html
State Adoption Exchange/Photolisting Service:
http://www.mare.org/

Minnesota Department of Human Services
http://www.dhs.state.mn.us/
Adoption and Foster Care Information:
http://www.dhs.state.mn.us/childint/programs/Adoption/default.htm
http://www.dhs.state.mn.us/childint/programs/fostercare/default.htm

State Adoption Exchange/Photolisting Service:
http://www.mnadopt.org

Mississippi Department of Human Services
http://www.mdhs.state.ms.us/
Adoption and Foster Care Information:
http://www.mdhs.state.ms.us/fcs_adopt.html
http://www.mdhs.state.ms.us/fcs_foster.html
State Adoption Exchange/Photolisting Service:
http://www.mdhs.state.ms.us/fcs_adopt.html#children

Missouri Department of Social Services
http://www.dss.state.mo.us/index.htm
Adoption and Foster Care Information:
http://www.dss.mo.gov/cd/adopt.htm
http://www.dss.mo.gov/cd/cfpp.htm
State Adoption Exchange/Photolisting Service:
http://www.dss.mo.gov/cd/adopt/index.htm

Montana Department of Public Health and Human Services
http://www.dphhs.state.mt.us/
Adoption and Foster Care Information:
http://www.dphhs.state.mt.us/services/programs_available/
foster_wmontana.htm
State Adoption Exchange/Photolisting Service:
http://www.adoptuskids.org/states/mt

Nebraska Health and Human Services
http://www.hhs.state.ne.us/
Adoption and Foster Care Information:
http://www.hhs.state.ne.us/chs/adp/adpindex.htm
http://www.hhs.state.ne.us/chs/foc/focindex.htm
State Adoption Exchange/Photolisting Service:
http://www.hhs.state.ne.us/adp/adpxchan.htm

Nevada Division of Child and Family Services
http://dcfs.state.nv.us
Adoption and Foster Care Information:

http://dcfs.state.nv.us/page33.html
http://dcfs.state.nv.us/page25.html
State Adoption Exchange/Photolisting Service:
http://dcfs.state.nv.us/page37.html

New Hampshire Department of Health and Human Services
http://www.dhhs.state.nh.us
Adoption and Foster Care Information:
http://www.nhfostercare.org
State Adoption Exchange/Photolisting Service:
http://www.adopt.org

New Jersey Department of Human Services
http://www.state.nj.us/humanservices/
Adoption and Foster Care Information:
http://www.state.nj.us/humanservices/adoption/adopt.html
http://www.njfostercare.org
State Adoption Exchange/Photolisting Service:
http://www.state.nj.us/humanservices/adoption/childframe.html

New Mexico Children, Youth and Families Department
http://www.cyfd.org
Adoption and Foster Care Information:
http://www.cyfd.org/adopt.htm
http://www.cyfd.org/foster.htm
State Adoption Exchange/Photolisting Service:
http://www.cyfd.org/adopt_categories.htm

New York Department of Family Assistance
http://www.dfa.state.ny.us
Adoption and Foster Care Information:
http://www.ocfs.state.ny.us/adopt/
http://www.ocfs.state.ny.us/main/fostercare/
State Adoption Exchange/Photolisting Service:
http://www.ocfs.state.ny.us/adopt/internet/InternetPhotoinq.asp

North Carolina Department of Health and Human Services
http://www.dhhs.state.nc.us/

Adoption and Foster Care Information:
http://www.dhhs.state.nc.us/dss/adopt
State Adoption Exchange/Photolisting Service:
http://www.dhhs.state.nc.us/dss/adopt

North Dakota Department of Human Services
http://www.state.nd.us/humanservices/
Adoption and Foster Care Information:
http://www.state.nd.us/humanservices/services/childfamily/adoption/
http://www.state.nd.us/humanservices/services/childfamily/fostercare/
State Adoption Exchange/Photolisting Service:
http://www.adopt.org

Ohio Department of Job and Family Services
http://jfs.ohio.gov/
Adoption and Foster Care Information:
http://jfs.ohio.gov/factsheets/Adoption.pdf
http://jfs.ohio.gov/factsheets/FosterCare.pdf
State Adoption Exchange/Photolisting Service:
http://jfs.ohio.gov/oapl/index.htm

Oklahoma Department of Human Services
http://www.okdhs.org
Adoption and Foster Care Information:
http://www.okdhs.org/adopt
http://www.okdhs.org/fostercare
State Adoption Exchange/Photolisting Service:
http://www.adoptuskids.org/states/ok

Oregon Department of Human Services
http://www.dhs.state.or.us/children/
Adoption and Foster Care Information:
http://www.oregon.gov/DHS/children/adoption/
http://www.dhs.state.or.us/children/fostercare/overview.htm
State Adoption Exchange/Photolisting Service:
http://www.nwae.org/wait-or.html

Pennsylvania Department of Public Welfare

http://www.dpw.state.pa.us/
Adoption and Foster Care Information:
http://www.dpw.state.pa.us/Child/AdoptionFosterCare/003670363.htm
http://www.dpw.state.pa.us/Child/AdoptionFosterCare/003670365.htm
State Adoption Exchange/Photolisting Service:
http://www.adoptpakids.org
http://www.diakon-swan.org

Rhode Island Department for Children, Youth and Family Services
http://www.dcyf.state.ri.us
Adoption and Foster Care Information:
http://www.dcyf.ri.gov/adoption.htm
http://www.dcyf.ri.gov/foster.htm
State Adoption Exchange/Photolisting Service:
http://www.adoptionri.org/

South Carolina Department of Social Services
http://www.state.sc.us/dss/
Adoption and Foster Care Information:
http://www.state.sc.us/dss/adoption
http://www.state.sc.us/dss/foster/index.html
State Adoption Exchange/Photolisting Service:
http://www.adoptuskids.org/states/sc/search.html

South Dakota Department of Social Services
http://www.state.sd.us/social/social.html
Adoption and Foster Care Information:
http://www.state.sd.us/social/cps/adoption/index.htm
http://www.state.sd.us/social/cps/Fostercare/process.htm
State Adoption Exchange/Photolisting Service:
http://www.state.sd.us/social/cps/Adoption/index.htm

Tennessee Department of Children's Services
http://www.state.tn.us/youth
Adoption and Foster Care Information:
http://www.state.tn.us/youth/adoption/index.htm
http://www.state.tn.us/youth/foster/index.htm
State Adoption Exchange/Photolisting Service:

http://www.state.tn.us/youth/adoption/profilesstart.htm

Texas Department of Protective and Regulatory Services
http://www.tdprs.state.tx.us/
Adoption and Foster Care Information:
http://www.tdprs.state.tx.us/Site_Map/foster.asp
State Adoption Exchange/Photolisting Service:
http://www.tdprs.state.tx.us/adoption_and_foster_care/Child_Search/default.asp

Utah Department of Human Services
http://www.dhs.state.ut.us/
Adoption and Foster Care Information:
http://www.hsdcfs.utah.gov/adoption.htm
http://www.hsdcfs.utah.gov/foster_care.htm
State Adoption Exchange/Photolisting Service:
http://www.utdcfsadopt.org

Vermont Child Welfare and Youth Justice Division
http://www.projectfamily.state.vt.us/
Adoption and Foster Care Information:
http://www.state.vt.us/srs/
http://www.path.state.vt.us/cwyj/adoption/
State Adoption Exchange/Photolisting Service:
http://www.path.state.vt.us/cwyj/PINS.shtml

Virginia Department of Social Services
http://www.dss.state.va.us/
Adoption and Foster Care Information:
http://www.dss.state.va.us/family/adoption.html
http://www.dss.state.va.us/family/fostercare.html
State Adoption Exchange/Photolisting Service:
http://www.adoptuskids.org/states/va

Washington Department of Social and Health Services
http://www.wa.gov/dshs/
Adoption and Foster Care Information:
http://www1.dshs.wa.gov/ca/index.asp

http://www1.dshs.wa.gov/ca/fosterparents/index.asp
State Adoption Exchange/Photolisting Service:
http://www.nwae.org

West Virginia Department of Health and Human Resources
http://www.wvdhhr.org/
Adoption and Foster Care Information:
http://www.wvdhhr.org/oss/adoption
http://www.wvdhhr.org/bcf/
State Adoption Exchange/Photolisting Service:
http://www.wvdhhr.org/oss/adoption/wv_children.asp

Wisconsin Department of Health and Family Services
http://www.dhfs.state.wi.us/
Adoption and Foster Care Information:
http://www.dhfs.state.wi.us/children/adoption/index.htm
State Adoption Exchange/Photolisting Service:
http://www.wiadopt.org/

Wyoming Department of Family Services
http://dfsweb.state.wy.us
Adoption and Foster Care Information:
http://dfsweb.state.wy.us/adoption.html
http://dfsweb.state.wy.us/ProtectiveSvc/Programs/FosterCare/FosterParentHandbook.htm
State Adoption Exchange/Photolisting Service:
http://dfsweb.state.wy.us/CHILDSVC/UPDATES/ADOPTION/Tocadp.htm
http://www.adoptex.org

Appendix B

Parent Support Groups

The following list of parent support groups was compiled and provided by the North American Council on Adoptable Children (NACAC). Please visit their website (www.nacac.org) for the latest updates to this list.

Each of the groups has been alphabetized by state. The primary contact name (as of the time of this printing) and name of the group is followed by contact information for the group. Lastly, find the primary focus groups they are prepared to support.

- Andrea Wilson
  Cross Cultural Families of Native Children
  13212 106 Avenue
  Edmonton, AB T5N 1A3
  Phone: 780-461-0205/780-490-0405
  Fax: 780-466-8405
  E-mail: ccfonc@ecn.ab.ca
  Web site: www.ecn.ab.ca/ccfonc
  Post-Adoption, Foster Care, Native American/Canadian, Transracial/Transcultural, Guardianship

- Freda Williams
  Greater Birmingham Foster & Adoptive Parents Assoc
  PO Box 11926
  Birmingham, AL 35202-1926
  Phone: 205-655-1543
  Fax: 205-655-1543
  E-mail: Bamabison@aol.com
  Pre-Adoption, Post-Adoption, Foster Care

- Nancy Williams
  Families First
  3220 W. Folgers
  Phoenix, AZ 85027
  Phone: 623-582-4846/602-818-4650
  Fax: 602-582-4846
  E-mail: nancywill2@cox.net
  Post-Adoption, Foster Care, Special Needs, Agency

- Fred & Barbara Leiner
  United Community Caregivers
  9849 Glade Ave
  Chatsworth, CA 91311
  Phone: 818-998-4481
  Fax: 818-998-4204
  Web site: www.fosterparents.com
  Foster Care

- Anne Fitzpatrick
  San Diego Co Foster Parent Assn
  13451 Starridge St.
  Poway, CA 92064
  Phone: 619-748-4502/619-579-4900
  Fax: 619-579-4900/619-748-2458
  E-mail: FstrMom4U@aol.com
  Foster Care

- CA State Foster Parent Assn, Inc.
  PO Box 22772
  San Diego, CA 92192
  Phone: 858-552-0691
  Foster Care

- David & Faith Friedlander
  Kids & Families Together
  856 E. Thompson Blvd.
  Ventura, CA 93001
  Phone: 805-643-3734/805-643-1446
  Fax: 805-643-0271
  E-mail: connect@kidsandfamilies.org
  Web site: www.kidsandfamilies.org
  Post-Adoption, Foster Care, Transracial/Transcultural, Kinship Care

- Judy Holmes
  Help One Child
  Union Presbyterian Church, 858 University Ave.
  Los Altos, CA 94024
  Phone: 650-917-1210
  Fax: 650-917-5796
  Web site: www.Helponechild.org
  Pre-Adoption, Post-Adoption, Foster Care

- Laurie Tyrrell
  Placer County Foster/Adopt Parents Support Group
  11716 Enterprise Drive
  Auburn, CA 95603
  Phone: 530-823-7278/530-889-6794
  Fax: 530-886-6735
  Foster Care

- Leah Eneix
  Yuba-Sutter Foster Adoptive Parent Association
  2785 Plute Rd
  Marysville, CA 95901
  Phone: 530-743-8437
  Fax: 530-634-3850
  E-mail: leneix@yccd.edu
  Foster Care

- Todd Goin
  Foster & Adoptive Parent Association of Larimer County
  8320 Firethorn Drive
  Loveland, CO 80538
  Phone: 970-669-3047
  Fax: 970-669-0674
  E-mail: Toddg@verinet.com
  Web site: www.lcfpa.org
  Foster Care

- Arlene Walsh
  Connecticut Assn of Foster and Adoptive Parents
  2189 Silas Deane Hwy.
  Rocky Hill, CT 06067
  Phone: 203-335-2277/860-258-3400/800-861-8838
  Fax: 860-258-3410

E-mail: arlene.walsh@cafap.com
Web site: www.cafap.com
Foster Care, Post-Adoption, Pre-Adoption

- Cynthia Franklin
  CT Foster & Adoptive Parents Assn
  2139 Silas Deane Hwy.
  Rocky Hill, CT 06067
  Phone: 860-347-8389/860-258-3400
  Fax: 860-258-3410
  E-mail: cafap@snet.com
  Web site: www.instantweb.com/~cafap
  Pre-Adoption, Post-Adoption, Foster Care

- Stephen J. Williams
  Pinellas Council on Adoptable Children
  3861 38th Street South
  St. Petersburg, FL 33711
  Phone: 727-410-1978
  Fax: 727-866-8963
  E-mail: stepspence@aol.com
  Post-Adoption, Foster Care, African American/Canadian, Pre-Adoption,
  Transracial/Transcultural, Single Parent, Kinship Care, Special Needs

- Sharon Meyer
  The Foundation for Large Families
  811 Lakeshore Blvd
  St. Cloud, FL 34760
  Phone: 407-892-6951
  E-mail: hvnsgate@cfl.rr.com
  Web site: www.geocities.com/largefamilies2001
  Pre-Adoption, Post-Adoption, Foster Care, Guardianship

- Trudy Petkovich
  DCF
  21731 SW 97 Ct.
  Miami, FL 33190
  Phone: 305-233-7081/866-330-8119
  E-mail: jpetkov248@aol.com
  Web site: www.kidsfpa.org
  Post-Adoption, Foster Care, Transracial/Transcultural, Kinship Care, Special
  Needs,

- Cheryl McDunnell
  Adoptive & Foster Parent Assn of Effingham County
  528 Williams St
  Rincon, GA 31326
  Phone: 912-826-1851
  Fax: 509-275-6111
  E-mail: cmcdun@cs.com
  Post-Adoption, Foster Care, Special Needs

- Marsha Clark
  Douglas County Adoptive/Foster Parent Association
  PO Box 1135
  Douglasville, GA 30133
  Phone: 770-947-7425
  Fax: 770-489-3035
  E-mail: Familymaker@adoption.com
  Primary Type of Group
  Foster Care

- Debbie Hoyt
  Iowa Connects
  149-35th Pl
  Runnells, IA 50237
  Phone: 515-966-2419/515-966-2565
  Fax: 515-462-2024
  E-mail: iaconnects@aol.com
  Web site: www.hometown.ad.com/iaconnects/myhomepage.html
  Pre-Adoption, Post-Adoption, Foster Care, Special Needs

- LSS Foster Parent Support Group
  525 SW 5th, Ste E
  Des Moines, IA 50309
  Phone: 641-271-7309
  Foster Care

- Mike & Christie McGuire
  North Central Foster Parent Assoc.
  2315 Rake Ave.
  Garner, IA 50438
  Phone: 641-923-2618
  Foster Care

- Patricia Cirks
  Children & Families of IA
  Fort Dodge Office, 1728 Central Ave., #10
  Fort Dodge, IA 50501-4200
  Phone: 641-573-2193
  Foster Care

- Kris & Greg Vierkant
  1722 E. Clark
  Charles City, IA 50616
  Phone: 641-228-7971
  Foster Care

- Nancy & Paul Magnall
  Iowa Foster and Adoptive Parents Association
  2004 11th St., SE
  Waverly, IA 50677
  Phone: 319-352-2197
  Fax: 319-352-8581
  E-mail: magnall_ifapa@msn.com
  Foster Care

- Dianna Seedorff
  Black Hawk Co Foster Parent Sup Group
  108 Sunset Lane
  Elk Run Heights, IA 50707
  Phone: 319-233-4285
  E-mail: dsl4852@cedarnet.org
  Foster Care, Pre-Adoption, Post-Adoption

- Mary Hart
  Lakes Area Foster & Adoptive Parents
  PO Box 515
  Estherville, IA 51334-0515
  Phone: 712-362-5608
  Fax: 712-362-7254
  E-mail: mary.hart@youthservices.com
  Foster Care, Pre-Adoption

- Dawn Luetje
  Lutheran Social Services.
  105 S. 7th St.

Denison, IA 51442
Phone: 712-263-9341
Fax: 712-263-6061
E-mail: dluetje@lssia.org
Foster Care

- Jan Shelman
  Des Moines/Henry/Louisa Support Group.
  2155-120th St.
  Windfield, IA 52659
  Phone: 319-254-2223
  E-mail: jshelman@younghouse.org
  Foster Care

- Tina Snyder & Denise McLoughlin
  Twin City Foster Parent Association
  201 W. 2nd St., PO Box 176
  Tampico, IL 61283
  Phone: T:815-626-8721 D:815-438-2065
  Fax: 815-438-2065
  E-mail: tnsnyder@theramp.net, ddm1050@hotmail.com
  Web site: tc-fpa.cityslide.com
  Foster Care, Guardianship

- Donsetta Blakely
  Northeast Area Foster/Adoptive
  6616 S. Washtenaw Ave
  Chicago, IL 60629
  Phone: 773-778-7445
  Fax: 773-778-9004
  E-mail: CHI4949@aol.com
  Pre-Adoption, Post-Adoption, Foster Care

- Elyse Flack
  Stars of David
  3175 Commercial Ave., #100
  Northbrook, IL 60062
  Phone: 847-433-5860/847-509-9929/800-STAR349
  E-mail: Starsdavid@aol.com
  Web site: www.starsofdavid.org
  Pre-Adoption, Jewish, Post-Adoption, Foster Care, Transracial/Transcultural,

International Adoption, Single Parent, Gay/Lesbian, Search and Reunion, Special Needs, Infertility, Adoptee

- Pamela Robbins
  Foster Children of Johnson County, Inc.
  827 N. Arroyo Dr
  Olathe, KS 66061
  Phone: 913-768-1840
  E-mail: pamrob@comcast.net
  Foster Care

- Harold & Julie Thorne
  PO Box 14
  Hoisington, KS 67544
  Phone: 316-653-4340
  E-mail: hlthorne@yahoo.com
  Foster Care

- Georgie Haman
  Family Enrichment Center
  1105 US 31W Bypass
  Bowling Green, KY 42101
  Phone: 866-842-9032
  Fax: 270-842-5831
  E-mail: adoptfec@bellsouth.net
  Web site: thefamilyenrichmentcenter.com
  Pre-Adoption, Post-Adoption, Foster Care, Single Parent, Kinship Care, Special Needs

- Margie Snell
  Region IX Foster & Adoptive Care Assn
  37245 Highway 10
  Franklinton, LA 70438
  Foster Care

- Deborah Byrd
  DC Metro Foster & Adoptive Parent Assn
  7226 Easy St
  Temple Hills, MD 20748
  Phone: 301-449-1061/301-279-3378
  Fax: 301-449-5911/301-449-5911

E-mail: deborah_byrd@mcpsmd.org
Foster Care

- Mildred Stewart
  Prince George's County Foster Parent Assn
  11809 Cleaver Dr
  Mitchville, MD 20721
  Phone: 301-249-2748
  Fax: 301-249-8756
  E-mail: beasleystewart@hotmail.com
  Foster Care

- ME Foster Parent Assn
  PO Box 834
  Waterville, ME 04903-0834
  Phone: 207-872-2265
  Foster Care, Pre-Adoption, Post-Adoption

- Bev Travis
  Clinton County Council Foster/Adoptive Youth Support Group
  MI 48835
  Phone: 989-682-4731
  E-mail: bjtravis@journey.com
  Foster Care

- Doug & Phyllis Lewis
  Midland County Foster Adoptive Network
  3100 Shreeve
  Midland, MI 48664
  Phone: 989-835-8738
  Fax: 989-835-4102
  E-mail: dougskids@chartermi.net
  Pre-Adoption, Post-Adoption, Foster Care

- Charles Stutts
  Spaulding for Children
  16250 Northland Dr., #120
  Southfield, MI 48075
  Phone: 248-443-7080
  Fax: 248-443-7099
  E-mail: sfc@spaulding.org

Web site: www.spaulding.org
Foster Care

- Karen Pitschka
  Hennepin County Foster Care Assn
  3347 Georgia Ave., N
  Crystal, MN 55427
  Phone: 763-537-7615
  Fax: 763-537-7615
  E-mail: karenpsl@aol.com
  Foster Care

- Melanie Sheetz
  Foster and Adoptive Care Coalition
  111 N. 7th Street, 6th Floor
  St. Louis, MO 63101
  Phone: same/314-340-7722
  Fax: 314-340-7754
  E-mail: melaniesheetz@foster-adopt.org
  Web site: www.foster-adopt.org
  Pre-Adoption, Post-Adoption, Foster Care, Kinship Care

- Millie Smith
  Parkland Foster & Adoptive Families
  408 N. Allen St.
  Bonne Terre, MO 63628
  Phone: 573-358-3512
  Fax: 573-756-6007
  E-mail: milcar@jcn.net
  Foster Care

- Edwin & Selma Shelton
  Foster & Adoptive Parents of Mid-MO
  7701 Cedar Hills Rd
  Ashland, MO 65010
  Phone: 573-657-9652
  Fax: 573-657-9656
  Foster Care, Post-Adoption, Pre-Adoption

- James & Lissa McKenna
  MO Foster Care & Adoption Assn
  PO Box 277

Cape Fair, MO 65624
Phone: 417-538-4362
Fax: 417-538-2604
E-mail: d.j.jim@interlinc.net
Foster Care

- Lori Ross
  Midwest Foster Care &, Adoption Association, Inc.
  8511 E. 21st St.
  Kansas City, MO 64014
  Phone: 816-224-4559/816-350-0215
  Fax: 816-461-7108
  E-mail: rross600@aol.com
  Web site: www.kidpros.com
  Pre-Adoption, Foster Care, Kinship Care, Single Parent

- Sylvia Sessions
  S. MS Foster & Adoptive Parent Support Group
  901 Union Rd
  Tylertown, MS 39667
  Phone: 601-876-6986
  Fax: 601-876-6978
  E-mail: magnum03@netdoor.com
  Web site: taz0306@bellsouth.net
  Foster Care

- Becky Mathis
  MS Foster & Adoptive Parents Assn
  PO Box 3451
  Meridian, MS 39303
  Phone: 601-776-5245/800-529-2210
  Fax: 601-776-6994/601-797-7929
  E-mail: mfapa@netdoor.com
  Foster Care, Pre-Adoption, Post-Adoption

- Janice Huff
  Family Matters of Jackson
  2062 Suzanne Dr
  Raymond, MS 39154
  Phone: 601-371-1165/601-853-5684
  Pre-Adoption, Post-Adoption, Foster Care, African American/Canadian,

Transracial/Transcultural, Single Parent, Kinship Care, Guardianship, Special Needs, Agency

- Dianne & Jerry Gore
  MS Adoption Foster Parent Group
  PO Box 4055
  Brandon, MS 39047
  Phone: 601-829-1095/601-992-4044
  Fax: 601-992-4144
  E-mail: princessdia@aol.com
  Pre-Adoption, Post-Adoption, Foster Care, African American/Canadian, Transracial/Transcultural, Single Parent, Special Needs

- Melody Blendu
  Yellowstone Valley Foster, & Adoptive Assn
  1740 Augsburg Dr.
  Billings, MT 59105
  Phone: 406-245-7543
  Fax: 406-259-0761
  E-mail: mblendu@hotmail.com
  Foster Care, Pre-Adoption, Post-Adoption, African American/Canadian, Transracial/Transcultural, Kinship Care, Guardianship, Agency

- Maryanne Sigmund & Craig Cook
  Hearts & Homes/MT DPHHS
  PO Box 254
  Manhattan, MT 59773
  Phone: 406-284-3095/406-585-8544
  Foster Care

- Ann A. Dodd
  Adoptive Parents Together
  9700 Wardlow Court
  Matthews, NC 28235
  Phone: 704-844-0432/704-376-7180x123
  Fax: 704-376-0904
  E-mail: annd@thefamilycenter.net
  Foster Care, Special Needs, Agency

- Robert & Vickie Thu
  Foster/Adopt Support Team
  2534-87th Ave., SE

Jamestown, ND 58401
Phone: 701-252-7512
E-mail: bob_thu@msn.com
Web site: http://zip.tp/bobthu
Pre-Adoption, Post-Adoption, Foster Care, Single Parent, International Adoption

- Sue Fisher
  Sierra Assn of Foster Families
  8700 Osage Rd.
  Reno, NV 89506
  Phone: 775-677-9381
  Fax: 775-677-9379
  E-mail: flatftsu21@aol.com
  Pre-Adoption, Post-Adoption, Foster Care, Native American/Canadian, Transracial/Transcultural, Special Needs

- Chinwe Okoye
  Urban League of Rochester
  265 N. Clinton Ave
  Rochester, NY 14605
  Phone: 716-325-6530 x-3053
  Fax: 716-325-4864
  E-mail: cokoye@ulr.org
  Post-Adoption, Foster Care

- Shirvy McBride
  Child Development Foster & Adoptive Parents Assn.
  200 Cozine Ave., Apt. 6J
  Brooklyn, NY 11207
  Phone: 718-257-6424
  Fax: 718-257-6424
  E-mail: cdfapa@aol.com
  Pre-Adoption, Foster Care, Special Needs

- Payal Dalal
  Circle of Support
  150 William Street, 5th Floor
  New York, NY 10038
  E-mail: Payal.Dalal@dfa.state.ny.us
  Web site: www.circleofsupport.org
  Foster Care

- Sam & Barbara Pitkowsky
  New York Adoptive Parents Committee
  254 Seaman's Ave
  New York, NY 10034
  Phone: 212-942-9708/212-304-8479
  Fax: 212-304-8479
  E-mail: samapc@aol.com
  Web site: www.adoptiveparents.org
  Pre-Adoption, Post-Adoption, Foster Care

- Judith Ashton
  New York State Citizens' Coalition, for Children, Inc.
  410 East Upland Rd
  Ithaca, NY 14850
  Phone: 607-272-0034
  Fax: 607-272-0035
  E-mail: jashton@nysccc.org
  Web site: www.nysccc.org
  Pre-Adoption, Post-Adoption, Foster Care, African American/Canadian, Asian/Pacific Islander, Latino/Hispanic, Native American/Canadian, Transracial/Transcultural, International Adoption, Single Parent, Gay/Lesbian, Kinship Care, Special Needs, Agency,

- Ellien Santana
  CWSN Parents Assoc
  1461 E. 59th St.
  Brooklyn, NY 11234
  Phone: 347-531-6974
  E-mail: cwsnpa@aol.com
  Foster Care, Pre-Adoption, Post-Adoption

- Lisa Maynard
  Adoption Resource Network, Inc.
  10 Rollingwood Dr
  Pittsford, NY 14534
  Phone: 585-385-6899/585-586-9586
  Fax: 585-586-9586
  E-mail: lisa_maynard@arni.org
  Web site: www.arni.org
  Pre-Adoption, Post-Adoption, Foster Care, International Adoption, Special Needs

- Helen Moyer
  Madison County Foster & Adoptive Parents
  1659 Glenwood Ave
  Oneida, NY 13421
  Phone: 315-361-4921
  E-mail: Rmoyer1@twcny.rr.com
  Web site: www.fafss.org
  Foster Care

- Dawn & Edward Corrigan
  Foster & Adoptive Family Support Services
  2 Lowell Dr.
  New Hartford, NY 13413
  Phone: 315-724-2989
  Fax: 315-724-4407
  E-mail: dac2547@aol.com
  Web site: www.fafss.org
  Foster Care

- Augusta & Naomi Bell
  Edwin Gould Foster and Adoptive Parents, Inc.
  15-19 W. 110th St., #33
  New York, NY 10026
  Phone: 212-456-5150/212-939-2500
  Fax: 212-426-9116
  E-mail: egfapa@aol.com
  Foster Care, Kinship Care, Special Needs, Post-Adoption

- Diane M. Fegley
  Seneca Co Foster & Adoptive Parent Support Group
  PO Box 690
  Waterloo, NY 13165-0690
  Phone: 315-539-1861
  Foster Care

- Ann Marie BreMiller
  Greene County Foster & Adoptive Parent Assn
  380 Cairo Junction Rd
  Catskill, NY 12414
  Phone: 518-943-9577
  E-mail: jashco3@aol.com
  Foster Care

- Randy Smith
  Fulton Co Foster and Adoptive Parent Assoc
  17 Poole Ave.
  Gloversville, NY 12078
  Phone: 518-736-5511
  E-mail: randys@superior.net
  Post-Adoption, Foster Care

- Dot Erickson
  Ohio Family Care Assn
  PO Box 82185
  Columbus, OH 43202
  Phone: 614-268-7776
  Fax: 614-262-7004
  E-mail: ofca@aol.com
  Web site: www.ohiofamilycareassoc.org
  Post-Adoption, Foster Care

- Gloria Rodriguez-Milord
  Beech Acres Foster & Adoptive Parents
  6881 Beechmont Ave.
  Cincinnati, OH 45230
  Phone: 513-232-3201/513-231-6630x224
  E-mail: gmilord@beecharcres.org
  Foster Care, Special Needs, Agency

- Cindy Griffin
  Life RAFFT (Raising Adoptive & Foster Families Together)
  13760 Old State Road
  Middlefield, OH 44024
  E-mail: ccbbcm@aol.com
  Post-Adoption, Foster Care, Transracial/Transcultural, International Adoption, Single Parent, Special Needs

- Valarie Howard
  Family Ties One Church One Child Family Support
  3129 N. Martin Luther King Blvd
  Oklahoma City, OK 73111
  Phone: 405-425-8501/405-424-0225
  Fax: 405-424-0975
  E-mail: 1church1child@sbcglobal.net
  Web site: www.onechurchonechildokla.com

Pre-Adoption, Post-Adoption, Foster Care, Kinship Care, African American/
Canadian

- Maureen Cech
Children's Aid Society of Ottawa-Carleton
1602 Telesat Court
Gloucester, ON K1B 1B1
Phone: 613-725-1744/613-747-7800 x-2628
Fax: 613-747-4456
E-mail: mcech@casott.on.ca
Web site: www.casott.on.ca
Pre-Adoption, Foster Care

- Marlene Kasbee
Family Support Group
1733 Locust Rd
Sewickley, PA 15143
Phone: 412-366-7113
E-mail: marleenk@icubed.com
Pre-Adoption, Post-Adoption, Foster Care, Special Needs

- Luisa Prichard
The Children's Institute, Project STAR
2310 7th Ave
Beaver Falls, PA 15010
Phone: 724-847-2330
Fax: 724-847-7895
E-mail: lpr@the-institute.org
Pre-Adoption, Post-Adoption, Foster Care, African American/Canadian,
Asian/Pacific Islander, Latino/Hispanic, Transracial/Transcultural, Interna-
tional Adoption, Single Parent, Kinship Care, Guardianship, Special Needs,
Agency

- Sandi Fisher
Foster & Adoptive Families of R.I.
PO Box 629
West Kingston, RI 02892
Phone: 401-783-5864/401-783-1738
Foster Care, Post-Adoption, Pre-Adoption, Special Needs

- Gail Groomster
SC Council on Adoptable Children

2005 Hampton St., Ste. F
Columbia, SC 29204
Phone: 803-865-1949/803-256-2622
Fax: 803-256-2767
E-mail: gail-coac@sc.rr.com
Pre-Adoption, Post-Adoption, Foster Care

- Carl Brown
  South Carolina Foster/Adoptive Parents Assn
  PO Box 39
  Elgin, SC 29045
  Phone: 803-865-2020
  Fax: 803-865-2020
  E-mail: cbrown39@aol.com
  Foster Care

- Saskatchewan Foster Families Assn
  2343 Broad St.
  Regina, SK S4P 1Y9
  Phone: 306-565-2880
  Fax: 306-347-8268
  E-mail: sffa@sk.sympatico.ca
  Foster Care

- Betty Hastings
  TN Foster and Adoptive Care Assn
  40 Foust Ln.
  Hollow Rock, TN 38342
  Phone: 731-986-5316
  Fax: 731-986-2386
  E-mail: bettyh@aeneas.net
  Web site: www.tfaca.org
  Foster Care

- Terri Zelasko
  Tarrant County Foster Parents
  TX 76115
  E-mail: terrizelasko@hotmail.com
  Web site: www.foster.itgo.com
  Pre-Adoption, Foster Care

- Luis F. Fernandez
  El Paso Foster & Adoptive Parent Assoc., Inc.
  10409 Bywood Dr
  El Paso, TX 79935
  Phone: 915-591-9352
  E-mail: epfpa@netscape.net
  Post-Adoption, Foster Care, Latino/Hispanic

- Marcia Hookie
  Foster and Adoptive Parents of Collin County
  PO Box 1544
  Allen, TX 75013
  Phone: 972-359-1959/972-359-1959
  E-mail: mhookie@mindspring.com
  Pre-Adoption, Post-Adoption, Foster Care, Single Parent

- Jamie Fiore
  Lutheran Family Services of VA
  PO Box 3232
  Hampton, VA 23663-0044
  Phone: 757-496-3754/757-722-4707x32
  Fax: 757-722-0898
  E-mail: jfiore@lfsva.org
  Web site: www.lfsva.org
  Pre-Adoption, Post-Adoption, Foster Care, Special Needs

- Charlotte Gaquerel
  Fredericksburg Area Foster & Forever Families
  308 Hanover St
  Fredericksburg, VA 22401
  Phone: 540-786-8729
  E-mail: gagw@aol.com
  Web site: www.umfs.org
  Single Parent, Post-Adoption, Foster Care, Special Needs, Transracial/Transcultural, International Adoption

- Maureen Oswald
  Fostering Adoptive Families
  119 Terrybrook Dr.
  Charlottesville, VA 22801
  Phone: 804-973-2981/434-973-2981
  Fax: 540-438-8467

E-mail: mmo8484@aol.com
Web site: www.groups.yahoo.com/group/adoption-preservation
Post-Adoption, Foster Care, Special Needs, Single Parent, International Adoption

- Kristen Brement
FACTS of Waynesboro, Staunton & Augusta County
213 Seybert Ave.
Waynesboro, VA 22980
Phone: 540-949-0974/540-949-0974
Fax: 540-438-8467
E-mail: ksb@intelos.net
Post-Adoption, Foster Care, International Adoption, Single Parent, Special Needs

- Vicky McKinney
FAS Family Resource Inst.
8607 24th Ave.
Tacoma, WA 98036
Phone: 253-539-0597/253-531-2878/800-999-3429
Fax: 253-531-2668
E-mail: vicfas@hotmail.com
Web site: www.fetalalcoholsyndrome.org
Pre-Adoption, Post-Adoption, Foster Care, African American/Canadian, Asian/Pacific Islander, Latino/Hispanic, Native American/Canadian, Transracial/Transcultural, International Adoption, Single Parent, Gay/Lesbian, Kinship Care, Special Needs

- Ande Kerschner
Friends in Adoption
PO Box 659
Auburn, WA 98071
Phone: 206-264-5136
E-mail: info@friends-in-adoption.org
Web site: http://friends-in-adoption.org
Pre-Adoption, Post-Adoption, International Adoption, Foster Care, Single Parent

- Anne Rankin
WI Foster and Adoptive Parent Assn, Inc.
7057 S. Lasch Ln
Lake Nebagamon, WI 54849

Phone: 715-374-2180
Fax: 715-374-2137
E-mail: varankin@discover-net.net
Foster Care, Post-Adoption, Pre-Adoption, Agency

- Jim Rice
  United Foster Parent Assn of Greater Milwaukee
  2333 N 60th St
  Wauwatosa, WI 53210
  Phone: 414-456-0631
  Fax: 414-456-0676
  E-mail: ufpagm@aol.com
  Foster Care

- Mary Jane Proft
  Wisconsin Foster and Adoptive Parents Associations, Inc (WFAPA)
  N98 W15725 Shagbark Rd
  Germantown, WI 53022
  Phone: 262-251-4412/262-251-4461
  Fax: 262-251-2167
  E-mail: Adopt12@aol.com
  Web site: www.wfapa.org
  Foster Care

APPENDIX C

State-by-State Definition of Special Needs Child for Subsidies

Alabama

State Subsidy Contact Person

Michael Jordan
Department of Human Resources (DHR)
50 N. Ripley Street
Montgomery, AL 36130
Phone: 334-242-9500
Fax: 334-242-0939
Email: mwjordan@dhr.state.al.us

Alabama's legal definition of special needs is as follows:

A child is defined as having special needs if it is unlikely for him/her to be adopted by reason of one or more of the following conditions: (a) physical or mental disability; (b) emotional disturbance; (c) recognized high risk of physical or mental disease; (d) children eight years old and older; (e) sibling groups of three or more children placed together at the same time; and (f) a child of Black heritage age two or older.

Alaska

State Subsidy Contact Person

Tracy Spartz Campbell
Dept. of Health & Social Services
Office of Children's Services
P.O. Box 110630
Juneau, AK 99811
Office: 907-465-3209
Fax: 907-465-3397
E-mail: Tracy_Spartz-Campbell@health.state.ak.us
Web: http://hss.state.ak.us/ocs

Alaska's legal definition of special needs is as follows:

A "hard-to-place"/special needs child is defined as a minor who is not likely to be adopted by reason of: physical or mental disability, emotional disturbance, recognized high risk of physical or mental disease, age, membership in a sibling group, racial or ethnic factors, or any combination of these conditions.

Arizona

State Subsidy Contact Person

Angela Cause
Department of Economic Security (DES)
Admin. for Children, Youth & Families
1789 W. Jefferson, P.O. Box 6123-940A
Phoenix, AZ 85005
Phone: 602-542-5499; Fax: 602-542-3330
E-mail: Angela.Cause@mail.de.state.az.us

Arizona's legal definition of special needs is as follows:

One or more of the following conditions existed before the finalization of adoption: (a) physical, mental, or developmental disability; (b) emotional disturbance; (c) high risk of physical or mental disease; (d) high risk of developmental disability; (e) age of six or more years at the time of application for subsidy; (f) sibling relationship; (g) racial or ethnic factors; (h) high risk of severe emotional disturbance if removed from the care of relatives or foster parents; or (i) any combination of the special needs described here.

Arkansas

State Subsidy Contact Person

Rochell Parker
Division of Children and Family Services (DCFS)
626 Donaghey Plaza South
P.O. Box 1437, Slot 808
Little Rock, AR 72203
Phone: 501-682-8462; Fax: 501-682-8094
E-mail: rochelle.parker@mail.state.ar.us

Arkansas' legal definition of special needs is as follows:

A special needs child is defined in Arkansas as a child who is free for adoption and has severe medical or psychological needs that require ongoing rehabilitation or treatment. Other children may be eligible for adoption assistance under this category if they belong to a group of children for whom the Division does not have an adequate resource of approved applicants to provide a pool of available waiting adoptive families. These children include:

(a) Caucasian child who is nine years of age or older;
(b) a healthy child of color who is two years of age or older;
(c) a child who is a member of a sibling group of three or more children being placed together and the child is:

- legally free for adoption with parental rights terminated

- under eighteen years old and whose adoption has not been finalized prior to approval of the subsidy.

California

State Subsidy Contact Person

Ms. Ty Starks Morgan
Eligibility & Funding/Rates Policy
Department of Social Services (DSS)

744 P Street, M.S. 29-12
Sacramento, CA 95814
Phone: 951-782-6600
Fax: 951-782-4985
E-mail: ty.starks@dss.ca.gov

California's legal definition of special needs is as follows:

The child has at least one of the following characteristics that are barriers to his or her adoption without subsidy:

a. Adoptive placement without financial assistance is unlikely because of membership in a sibling group that should remain intact, or by virtue of race, ethnicity, color, language, age of 3 years or older, or parental background of a medical or behavioral nature that can be determined to adversely affect the development of the child; and/or

b. Adoptive placement without financial assistance is unlikely because the child has a mental, physical, emotional, or medical disability that has been certified by a licensed professional competent to make an assessment and operating within the scope of his or her profession.

Colorado

State Subsidy Contact Person

Sharen Ford
Department of Human Services (DHS)
1575 Sherman Street
Denver, CO 80203-1714
Phone: 303-866-3197
Fax: 303-866-5563
E-mail: sharen.ford@state.co.us

Colorado's legal definition of special needs is as follows:

A "special need" is one or more of the following special, unusual, or significant factors that act as a barrier to the child's adoption:

1. Physical disability (such as hearing, vision or physical impairment; neurological conditions; disfiguring defects; and, heart defects);

2. Mental retardation (such as developmental delay or disability, perceptual or speech/language disability or a metabolic disorder);

3. Developmental disability resulting in educational delays or significant learning processing difficulties;

4. Educational disability which qualified for Section 504 of the Rehabilitation Act of 1973 or special educational services;

5. Emotional disturbance;

6. Hereditary factors that have been documented by a physician or psychologist;

7. High risk children (such as HIV-positive, drug-exposed, or alcohol-exposed in utero); or

8. Other conditions that act as a serious barrier to the child's adoption. Conditions may include but are not limited to a healthy child over the age of seven or a sibling group that should remain intact and medical conditions likely to require further treatment.

Connecticut

State Subsidy Contact Person

Sandy Matlack
Department of Children and Families (DCF)
Division of Family and Adoption Services
505 Hudson Street
Hartford, CT 06105
Phone: 860-550-6392
Fax: 860-566-6726
E-mail: Sandy.Matlack@po.state.ct.us

Connecticut's legal definition of special needs is as follows:

Connecticut defines a special needs child as a child who is difficult to place in an adoptive home because of one or more of the following conditions: (a) over the age of two, and there are racial/ethnic barriers to adoption; (b) physical or mental disability or serious emotional maladjustment; (c) over the age of eight; (d) member of a sibling group that includes two or more children who should be, or remain in, the same adoptive home; or (e) recognized high risk of physical or mental disability.

Delaware

State Subsidy Contact Person

Ana Prosceno
DSCYF/Division of Family Services
1825 Faulkland Road
Wilmington, DE 19805
Work: 302-633-2661
Fax: 302-633-2652
E-mail: ana.prosceno@state.de.us

Delaware's legal definition of special needs is as follows:

There must exist with respect to the child a specific factor or condition that prohibits adoption without adoption assistance. These factors include, but are not limited to, the following: (a) age of the child (8 years or older); (b) membership in a minority race, or ethnic background; (c) membership in a sibling group to be adopted in the same placement; (d) mental or emotional conditions, verified by a psychologist, psychiatrist, or other qualified professional; or (e) medical condition, physical handicap, or disease which requires ongoing medical attention as verified by a physician.

District of Columbia

District Subsidy Contacts

Felicia Kraft
Child and Family Services Agency
Adoption Resources Program

400 6th St. SW, 3rd floor
Washington, DC 20002
Phone: 202-727-2377; Fax: 202-727-7709

Patricia Johnson
Child and Family Services Agency
Adoption Resources Program
400 6th St. SW, 3rd floor
Washington, DC 20002
Phone: 202-727-2377; Fax: 202-727-7709

District of Columbia's legal definition of special needs is as follows:

A child is considered to have special needs if they meet one or more of the following criteria: (a) physical, mental, or emotional handicapping condition; (b) 2 years of age or older; (c) developmentally delayed pre-school age child; or (d) member of a minority and/or birth assembled sibling group

Florida

State Subsidy Contact Person

Carol Hutcheson
Dept. of Children & Family Services (DCFS)
1317 Winewood Blvd., Bldg. 7
Tallahassee, FL 32301
Phone: 850-487-2383
Fax: 850-488-0751
E-mail: carol_hutcheson@dcf.state.fl.us

Florida's legal definition of special needs is as follows:

A special needs child is: (1) one who has established significant emotional ties with his or her foster parents; or (2) is not likely to be adopted because he or she is: (a) eight years of age or older; (b) mentally retarded; (c) physically or emotionally handicapped; (d) of black or racially mixed parentage; or (e) a member of a sibling group of any age.

Georgia

State Subsidy Contact Person

Gail Greer
DHR/Office of Adoptions
2 Peachtree St. NW, 3-323
Atlanta, GA 30303
Phone: 404-657-3558
Fax: 404-657-9498
E-mail: gmgreer@dhr.state.ga.us

Georgia's legal definition of special needs is as follows:

A child who is considered special needs is: (a) any child 8 years of age or older; (b) any child of Black heritage, 1 year of age or older; (c) members of a sibling group of three or more; (d) members of a sibling group of 2 where one is over the age of 8 or has another special need; (e) any child with documented physical, emotional, or mental problems or limitations.

Hawaii

State Subsidy Contact Person

Susan Ogami-VanCamp
Department of Human Services (DHS)
810 Richards St. Suite 400
Honolulu, HI 96813
Phone: 808-587-3168
Fax: 808-586-4806
E-mail: SOgami-VanCamp@dhs.hawaii.gov

Hawaii's legal definition of special needs is as follows:

A child who is legally freed for adoption but who cannot be placed with an adoptive parent without providing adoption assistance because of one or more of the following specific factors or conditions: (a) ethnic background; (b) age; (c) membership in a sibling group being adopted by the same family, not necessarily at the same time; (d) severe or chronic medical condition, physical, mental, or emotional disability; (e) at high risk for a severe or chronic medical condition, physical, mental, or emotional disability.

Idaho

State Subsidy Contact Person

Meri Brennan
Department of Health & Welfare
Division of Family and Children's Svcs.
P.O. Box 83720-5th floor
Boise, ID 83720-0036
Phone: 208-334-5700; Fax: 208-334-6664
E-mail: brennanm@idhw.state.id.us

Idaho's legal definition of special needs is as follows:

A child with special needs has the following characteristics: (a) physical, mental, emotional, or medical disability, or is at risk of developing such disability based on known information regarding the birth family and child's history; (b) age makes it difficult to find an adoptive home; (c) membership in a sibling group that must not be placed apart; or (d) establishment of such close emotional ties with a foster or relative family such that replacement is likely to be as traumatic to the child as removal from a biological family.

Illinois

State Subsidy Contact Person

June Dorn
Department of Children & Family Services (DCFS)
100 W. Randolph, Suite 6-100
Chicago, IL. 60601
Phone: (312) 814-6858
e-mail: Jdorn@idcfs.state.il.us

Illinois's legal definition of special needs is as follows:

Adoption assistance may be provided to those persons adopting children who are: (1) legally free for adoption; (2) residents of Illinois, and (3) who the Department has determined have special needs because of which it is reasonable to conclude that the child cannot be adopted unless adoption assistance is provided. A child shall not be considered to have special needs unless the Department has first determined that:

1. the child cannot or should not be returned to the home of his or her parents, as determined by: (a) a judicial adjudication that the child is abused, neglected or dependent or other judicial determination that there is probable cause to believe that a child is abused, neglected or dependent; and (b) a determination by the Department that the child is likely to suffer further abuse or neglect or will not be adequately cared for if returned to the parent(s); and

2. the child meets one of the following criteria: (a) has an irreversible or non-correctable physical, mental or emotional disability; or (b) has a physical, mental or emotional disability correctable through surgery, treatment, or other specialized services; or (c) is one year of age or older; or (d) is a member of a sibling group being adopted together where at least one child meets one of the above criteria, or; (e) is a child being adopted by adoptive parents who have previously adopted, with adoption assistance, another child(ren) born of the same mother or father; and

3. a reasonable, but unsuccessful, effort has been made to place the child with adoptive parents without providing adoption assistance and the prospective adoptive parents are either unwilling or unable to adopt the child without adoption assistance, as evidenced by a written statement from the adoptive parents. A documented search for alternative adoptive placements without adoption assistance shall be made unless the Department determines that such a search is not in the best interests of the child because the child has developed significant emotional ties with the prospective adoptive parents while in their foster care.

Indiana

State Subsidy Contact Person

Marcy Friedle
Indiana Adoption Subsidy Consultant
Department of Children's Services
402 W. Washington Street, W364 MS08
Indianapolis, IN 46204-2773
Phone: 317-232-4465
Fax: 317-232-4436
E-mail: Marcella.Friedle@fssa.in.gov

Indiana's legal definition of special needs is as follows:

A child must have one or more specific factors or conditions that preclude placement in an appropriate home without assistance payments. These specific factors are defined in detail as:

a. a child two years of age or older;

b. a child who is a member of a sibling group of two or more children of which at least one is two years of age or older and who will be placed with the sibling group in the same home;

c. a child with a medical condition or physical, mental, or emotional disability, or a recognized high risk of such condition or disability which would make the child difficult to place without assistance and which was determined and documented by a physician licensed to practice in Indiana or another state or territory.

  NOTE: If the special need is based solely on a medical condition or disability, correction or alleviation of the condition does not render the child ineligible for continued assistance benefits.

Iowa

State Subsidy Contact Person

Charlcie Carey
Department of Human Services (DHS)

1305 East Walnut
Hoover Bldg., 5th floor
Des Moines, IA 50319
Phone: 515-281-5358; Fax: 515-281-4597
E-mail: ccarey@dhs.state.ia.us

Iowa's legal definition of special needs is as follows:

A child is eligible for subsidy when s/he is under the guardianship of the state, county, or a licensed child placing agency immediately prior to the adoption, and is determined to be a child with special needs based on one or more of the following reasons: (1) the child has a medically diagnosed disability which substantially limits one or more major life activities, or requires professional treatment, assistance in self-care, or the purchase of special equipment; (2) the child has been determined to be mentally retarded by a qualified mental retardation professional; (3) the child has been determined by a qualified mental health professional to be at high risk of having mental retardation, or having an emotional disability as determined by a qualified mental health professional, or having a physical disability as determined by a physician; (4) the child has been diagnosed by a qualified mental health professional to have a psychiatric condition which impairs the child's intellectual or social functioning; (5) the child has a diagnosed behavioral or emotional disorder characterized by situationally inappropriate behavior which deviates substantially from behavior appropriate to the child's age and interferes significantly with the child's intellectual, social, and personal adjustment; (6) the child is age eight or over and Caucasian; (7) the child is a member of a minority race or ethnic group, or the child's biological parents are of different races; (8) the child is a member of a sibling group of three or more who are placed in the same adoptive home, or a sibling group of two if one of the children has special needs because of one of the above reasons.

NOTE: Examples of conditions which do not qualify a child as special needs (unless a qualified professional documents that the condition limits the child's activities severely) include: minor allergies, heart murmurs, upper respiratory infections, ear infections, and correctable physical handicaps.

Kansas

State Subsidy Contact Person

Mary Siefken
Social and Rehabilitation Services (SRS)
Children & Family Services
Docking State Office Building
915 SW Harrison, 5th Floor South
Topeka, KS 66612-1588
Phone: 785-368-8180
Fax: 785-368-8159
E-mail: mes@srskansas.org

Kansas' legal definition of special needs is as follows:

- The State has determined the child cannot be returned to the home of the parents and the child is legally free for adoption;

- The State has made reasonable efforts to place the child without assistance, unless the child is being adopted by a relative or foster parent; and

- It has been determined that, based on a specific factor or condition, it is reasonable to conclude that a child cannot be placed without adoption assistance. Specific factors may include, but are not limited to:

1. age—the child shall be twelve years of age or older if age is the only special needs factor or condition;

2. medical conditions or physical, mental, or emotional handicaps;

3. membership in a sibling group of two or more children adopted together, one of whom meets the special needs criteria. For sibling groups of two, at least one sibling must have another special needs condition. Sibling groups of three or more, being placed together, do not need to meet any other criteria; or

4. a family/genetic history indicating that the child may need medical treatment or therapy at various developmental milestones (e.g., fetal alcohol syndrome, sexual abuse, mental retardation).

Read more about the specific factors and conditions that affect a child's eligibility for adoption assistance.

Note: The presence of one or more of these factors does not, in and of itself, render a child a special needs child. It is the linking of one or more of these factors with the conclusion that it is reasonable to believe such child cannot be placed without providing adoption support. See attached sheet for details.

Note: When a child's eligibility for adoption subsidy is based on the high risk of developing a physical, development, or emotional disability, a monthly subsidy payment shall not be made unless and until the potential disability manifests itself as documented by an appropriate health care professionals, physician, psychiatrist, psychologist, clinical social worker, or diagnostic center.

Kentucky

State Subsidy Contact Person

Mike Grimes, Internal Policy Analyst
Dept. for Community Based Services
275 East Main Street, 3C-E
Frankfort, KY 40621
Phone: 502-564-2147
Fax: 502-564-5995
E-mail: mike.grimes@ky.gov

Kentucky's legal definition of special needs is as follows:

In order for a child to qualify for adoption assistance, three criteria must be met and the child must meet one or more of the special needs criteria.

1. The state shall determine that the child shall not be returned to the home of his parents (e.g., TPR).

2. The child shall have a specific special need.

3. A reasonable, but unsuccessful effort was made to place the child without providing adoption assistance (e.g. referral to SNAP (Special Needs Adoption) or out-of-state agency as there was no waiting family available, or con-

ditions exist which have made it impossible to place such a child in the past without adoption assistance.) This criteria need not be met when there are significant emotional ties with prospective parents while in their care as a foster child.

SPECIAL NEEDS CRITERIA

- Has a physical or mental disability;

- Has an emotional or behavioral disorder;

- Has a recognized risk of physical, mental or emotional disorder;

- Is a member of a sibling group in which the siblings are placed together;

- Has had previous adoption disruption or multiple placements;

- Is an African American child two (2) years old or older; or

- Is age seven (7) or older and has a significant emotional attachment or psychological tie to his/her foster family and the Cabinet has determined that it would be in the child's best interest to remain with the family.

Louisiana

State Subsidy Contact Person

Genita Hunter
Department of Social Services (DSS)
Office of Community Services
333 Laurel Street, P.O. Box 3318
Baton Rouge, LA 70821
Phone: 225-342-2844; Fax: 225-342-9087
E-mail: ghunter1@ocs.dss.state.la.us

Louisiana's legal definition of special needs is as follows:

Any one or combination of the following conditions making it difficult to place without subsidy: (a) white male, age 11 or older; (b) black male, infant or older; (c) white female, age 12 or older; (d) black female, age 5 or older; (e) ethnic background; (f) physical condition; (g) mental and/or emotional condition; (h) membership in a sibling group that should not be separated; or (i) high risk of developing future problems due to past and birth family history. Provisions for exceptions to the definition of a "special needs" child may be made on a case-by-case basis.

Maine

State Subsidy Contact Person

Susan Harris or Virginia Marriner
Department of Human Services (DHS)
221 State Street
Augusta, ME 04333
Phone: 207-287-5060
Fax: 207-287-5282
E-mail: susan.d.harris@maine.gov
E-mail: virginia.s.marriner@maine.gov
www.state.me.us/dhs/bcfs

Maine's legal definition of special needs is as follows:

The term "special needs" refers to one or more of the following characteristics: (a) physical, mental, or emotional handicap that makes placement difficult; (b) medical condition which makes placement difficult; (c) is a member of a sibling group that includes at least one member who is hard to place; (d) difficult to place because of age or race; (e) has been a victim of physical, emotional, or sexual abuse or neglect that places the child at risk for future emotional difficulties; (f) factors in the child's family background such as severe mental illness, substance abuse, prostitution, or genetic or medical conditions or illnesses that place the child at risk of future problems.

Maryland

State Subsidy Contact Person

Stephanie Johnson Pettaway
Department of Human Resources (DHR)
Social Services Administration

311 W. Saratoga Street
Baltimore, MD 21201
Phone: 410-767-7506
Fax: 410-333-0922
E-mail: spettawa@dhr.state.md.us

Maryland's legal definition of special needs is as follows:

To qualify on the basis of the child's special needs, the child shall be one for whom the local department or agency which holds guardianship has made reasonable efforts to find an adoptive family without subsidy, but has not been successful because of one or more of the following factors:

a.   Six years old and over, but not yet 18 years old;

b.   Race or ethnic background, as follows:
(i) The child's membership in a minority race or ethnic group alone does not qualify for subsidy,
(ii) Documentation in the child's records shall clearly indicate how the child's minority background, in addition to other special needs, prevented an adoptive placement without subsidy;

c.   Physical or mental disability or risk of it;

d.   Emotional disturbance;

e.   Membership in a sibling group; or

f.   Recognized high risk of physical or mental disease.

Massachusetts

State Subsidy Contact Person

Ronald A Seletsky, Subsidy Manager
Massachusetts Department of Social Services
24 Farnsworth Street
Boston, MA 02210

Phone: 617-748-2371 / 800-835-0838
Fax: 617-261-7437

Massachusetts's legal definition of special needs is as follows:

A child is a child with special needs if the Department determines that the child meets the following three criteria:

a.   The child cannot or should not be returned to the home of his parents.

b.   At least one of the following circumstances applies:

   1.   The child has one or more special needs as a result of a mental, emotional, or physical impairment, behavioral disorder, or medical condition that has been diagnosed by a licensed professional who is qualified to make the diagnosis.

   2.   The child is difficult to place for one or more of the following reasons:

      a.   The child is a member of a sibling group of two to be adopted together and one of the children is eight years of age or older;

      b.   The child is a member of a sibling group of three or more to be adopted together; or

      c.   The child is a member of an ethnic or cultural minority for whom reasonable, but unsuccessful, efforts to place the child in an adoptive home without subsidy were made and documented.

   3.   The child's birth and/or family history places the child at risk of having special needs but, due to the child's age, a reliable diagnosis cannot be made.

c.   Reasonable efforts have been made to place the child for adoption in the most appropriate home without providing adoption subsidy. The requirement to make such efforts may be waived for any child whose best interests would not be served by a new placement because the child has developed significant emotional or psychological ties with the pre-adoptive parent(s) while in the care of such parent(s), and the pre-adoptive parent(s) cannot adopt the child without adoption subsidy.

NOTE: If the reason for adoption subsidy is due to a physical or mental disability, emotional disturbance, or attachment issues, the social worker documents the condition by obtaining current reports and/or prognoses from the child's doctor, psychologist, therapist, or other appropriate medical professional.

Michigan

State Subsidy Contact Person

Kate Young
Family Independence Agency (FIA)
235 S. Grand Avenue, P. O. Box 30037
Lansing, MI 48909
Phone: 517-335-3525
Fax: 517-335-4019
Web: www.mfia.state.mi.us

Michigan's legal definition of special needs is as follows:

The minimum requirements for certification of eligibility for a state-funded support subsidy are: (a) the child has been in foster care for at least 4 months immediately prior to the certification request; (b) a reasonable effort has failed to locate a family willing to adopt without support subsidy or a particular family is determined to be the only placement in the child's best interest; (c) the certification request is filed before the child's eighteenth birthday; (d) certification is approved before the petition for adoption is filed.

In addition to these criteria, eligibility for federally funded Title IV-E adoption assistance requires the existence of specific factors or conditions because of which it is reasonable to conclude that the child in question cannot be placed without assistance. These specific factors or conditions may include: (a) aphysical, mental, or emotional handicap or condition; (b) membership in a sibling group of two or more being placed together; (c) membership in a minority or ethnic group; (d) an age factor (age 3 or more).

Minnesota

State Subsidy Contact Person

Gerry Yaeger
Department of Human Services (DHS)
444 Lafayette Road
St. Paul, MN 55155
Phone: 651-297-3910
Fax: 651-296-5430
E-mail: Gerry.E.Yaeger@state.mn.us

Minnesota's legal definition of special needs is as follows:

The child must have one or more of the following special needs:

1. The child is a member of a sibling group to be placed as one unit where at least one sibling is older than 15 months of age.

2. The child has documented physical, mental, emotional, or behavioral disabilities.

3. The child has a high risk of developing physical, mental, emotional, or behavioral disabilities.

Note: When an infant's eligibility for adoption assistance is based on the high risk of developing physical, mental, emotional, or behavioral disabilities, payments shall not be made under the adoption assistance agreement unless and until the potential disability manifests itself as documented by an appropriate health care professional.

Mississippi

State Subsidy Contact Person

Phoebe Clark
Department of Human Services
Family and Children Services
750 North State Street
Jackson, MS 39202
Phone: 601-359-4981; Fax: 601-359-4226

800-345-6347 (in state); 800-553-7545 (out of state)
E-Mail: pclark@mdhs.state.ms.us

Mississippi's legal definition of special needs is as follows:

A child must possess one or more of the following special needs: (a) physical disability; (b) mental disability (IQ of 70 or less); (c) developmental disability; (d) emotional disturbance; (e) membership in a sibling group of two or more who are placed together; (f) age 6 or older; (g) racial or ethnic factors; (h) medical condition(s); or (i) a history of abuse that puts a child at risk of having special needs.

Missouri

State Subsidy Contact Person

Amy Martin
DSS/Children's Division
615 Howerton Court
P.O. Box 88
Jefferson City, MO 65103-0088
Phone: 573-751-3171
Fax: 573-526-3971
E-mail: Amy.L.Martin@dss.mo.gov

Missouri's legal definition of special needs is as follows:

A child with special needs is defined as follows: (a) 5 years of age or older, and/or; (b) minority racial or ethnic heritage, and/or; (c) intellectually, emotionally, or physically handicapped, and/or; (d) requires placement with siblings, and/or; (e) has a condition (i.e., a state of health or behavior) which results in a guarded prognosis (although the child may appear normal) due to mental illness or retardation, drug usage by, or venereal disease of, the parents, and/or; (f) a history which includes circumstances such as long alternative care, incest, or social or genetic complications in the family background which provide other impediments to adoption.

Note: A child with an intellectual and/or emotional limitation must have the condition documented by appropriate professional evaluation before subsidy can be approved.

All children who have been in the custody or are currently in the custody of the Children's Division (CD) are considered to have special needs.

Montana

State Subsidy Contact Person

Lynda Korth
Department of Public Health & Human Services
Division of Child and Family Services
P.O. Box 8005, 1400 Broadway
Helena, MT 59604
Phone: 406-444-5919
Fax: 406-444-5956
E-mail: lkorth@state.mt.us

Montana's legal definition of special needs is as follows:

Child with special needs means a child who is under the placement and care responsibility of the State agency (DPHHS) or that of a Tribe with whom the State has a Title IV-E agreement, and:

1. the child has been defined as a "child with special needs" because he or she meets at least one of the following criteria:

    a. diagnosed as having a physical, mental, or emotional disability;

    b. recognized to be at high risk of developing a physical, mental or emotional disability;

    c. a member of a minority group;

    d. six years of age or older;

    e. a member of a sibling group to be placed together for adoption; and

2. the child is under 18 years of age at the time the subsidized adoption agreement is signed; and

3. the child is legally free for adoption and cannot or should not be returned to the home of his or his parent(s); and

4. adoptive placement is in the child's best interest; and

5. the State of Montana has determined that reasonable, but unsuccessful, efforts have been made to place the child with appropriate adoptive parents without a subsidy, except where it would be against the best interests of the child because of such factors as the existence of significant emotional ties with prospective adoptive parents while in the care of such parents as a foster child.

Nebraska

State Subsidy Contact Person

Mary Dyer
Department of Health and Human Services (HHS)
301 Centennial Mall South
Box 95044
Lincoln, NE 68509-5044
Phone: 402-471-9331
Fax: 402-471-9034
E-mail: mary.dyer@hhss.state.ne.us

Nebraska's legal definition of special needs is as follows:

There must be documentation of at least one of the following special needs: (a) age (if age is the only special need, children age seven or younger generally are not considered eligible); (b) membership in a sibling group of three or more to be placed together; (c) strong attachment to foster/adoptive parents by whom the child is to be adopted, so that breaking the attachment would be harmful to the child; (d) behavioral, emotional, physical, or mental handicap.

Nevada

State Subsidy Contact Person

Wanda Scott
Department of Human Services
Division of Child & Family Services, Adoptions
4220 S. Maryland Pkwy, Bldg B, Ste 300
Las Vegas, NV 89119
Phone: 702-486-7633
Fax: 702-486-7626
E-mail: wlscott@dcfs.state.nv.us

Nevada's legal definition of special needs is as follows:

There exists with respect to the child a specific factor or condition (such as ethnic background, age, or membership in a minority or sibling group, or the presence of factors such as medical condition or physical, mental, or emotional handicaps) because of which it is reasonable to conclude that such child cannot be placed with adoptive parents without providing adoption assistance.

a.   Child is 6 years of age or older if age is the only determining factor;

b.   Child is a member of a sibling group of two or more to be placed together, and at least one of the children is age 6 years old;

c.   Child has a diagnosed medical, physical, emotional, or mental disability or documented history of abuse/neglect which requires ongoing treatment; or

d.   Child belongs to a minority race or ethnic group and children of that group cannot be readily placed due to lack of placement resources.

New Hampshire

State Subsidy Contact Person

Cathy Atkins
Division for Children and Youth Services (DCYS) Adoption Unit
129 Pleasant St.
Concord, NH 03301
Phone: 603-271-4707

Fax: 603-271-4729
E-mail: catkins@dhhs.state.nh.us

New Hampshire's legal definition of special needs is as follows:

The child must be considered "hard-to-place" because of one or more of the following reasons: (a) physical or mental handicap; (b) emotional disturbance; (c) age (if age is the sole factor to be used in determining the need for an adoption subsidy, the child must be 6 or older); (d) membership in a sibling group of two or more who need to be placed together; (e) language barrier; (f) ethnic background, race, or color.

New Jersey

State Subsidy Contact Person

Mary Lou Sweeney
Department of Human Services
Division of Youth & Family Services
50 East State Street, CN 717
Trenton, NJ 08625
Phone: 609-633-3991; Fax: 609-984-5449

New Jersey's legal definition of special needs is as follows:

"Hard-to-place" child means any child who is reasonably expected not to be placed for adoption due to the lack of a prospective adoptive home for any of the following reasons: (1) Any medical or dental condition which will require repeated or frequent hospitalization or treatment; (2) Any physical handicap, by reason of physical defect or deformity, whether congenital or acquired by accident, injury or disease, which makes or may be expected to make a child totally or partially incapacitated for education or for remunerative occupation; (3) Any substantial disfigurement, such as the loss or deformation of facial features, torso, or extremities; (4) A diagnosed emotional or behavioral problem, psychiatric disorder, serious intellectual incapacity, or brain damage which seriously affects the child's ability to relate to his peers or authority figures, including but not limited to a developmental disability; (5) The child is one of a group of three or more siblings (including half-siblings) and it is considered necessary that the group be placed together, or the child is one of two siblings, one of whom meets the hard-to-place criteria; (6) The child is 10 years old or older; (7) The child is over two years of age and a member of an ethnic group for whom adoptive homes are not readily available; (8) The child is over five years of age and has been living with foster parents for at least 12 months and adoption by the foster parents is the most appropriate plan for the child. A child in this situation under five may be deemed hard-to-place if he or she is a member of an ethnic group for whom adoptive homes are not readily available; (9) Any other condition approved by the Director.

New Mexico

State Subsidy Contact Person

Emily Garcia
Dept. of Children, Youth & Families
Division of Protective Services
PERA Bldg. 216
P.O. Drawer 5160
Santa Fe, NM 87502
Phone: 505-827-8413
Fax: 505-827-8480

New Mexico's legal definition of special needs is as follows:

A child must meet one of the following criteria: (a) over age 5; (b) member of a minority ethnic race or background; (c) part of a sibling group of three or more children; (d) moderate to severe developmental, psychological, or physical disabilities/handicaps manifested before age 18.

New York

State Subsidy Contact Person

Bruce Bushart
Office of Children & Family Services
NYS Adoption Services
Capital View Office Park

52 Washington St.
Rensselaer, NY 12144
Phone: 518-474-9447
Fax: 518-486-6326

New York's legal definition of special needs is as follows:

Children under 21 who are handicapped or hard-to-place are eligible for subsidy.

The term "handicapped" refers to a child who possesses a specific physical, mental, or emotional condition or disability of such severity or kind which, in the opinion of the Office of Children and Family Services constitutes a significant obstacle to the child's adoption. Such conditions include, but are not limited to: (a) any medical or dental condition which will require repeated or frequent hospitalization, treatment or follow-up care; (b) any physical handicap, by reason of physical defect or deformity, whether congenital or acquired by accident, injury or disease, which makes or may be expected to make a child totally or partially incapacitated for education or for remunerative occupation; (c) any substantial disfigurement such as the loss or deformation of facial features, torso or extremities; or, (d) a diagnosed personality or behavioral problem, psychiatric disorder, serious intellectual incapacity or brain damage which seriously affects the child's ability to relate to his or her peers and/or authority figures, including mental retrdation or developmental disability.

[NOTE: The definition of "handicapped" is not all-inclusive.]

The term "hard-to-place" refers to a child, other than a handicapped child, who: (a) has not been placed for adoption within six months of the date his or her guardianship and custody were committed to the social services official; (b) has not been placed for adoption within six months from the date a previous adoption placement terminated; (c) meets any one of the following conditions—(1) the child is one of a group of two siblings who are free for adoption, and it is considered necessary that the group be placed together, and (i) at least one of the siblings is five years old or older, or (ii) at least one of the siblings is a member of a minority group, or (iii) at least one of the siblings is eligible for subsidy; (2) the child is one of a group of three or more siblings and it is considered necessary that the group be placed together; (3) the child is eight years old or older and is a member of a minority group; (4) the child is 10 years old or older; and (5) the child is hard-to-place with parents other than his or her present foster parents because he or she has been in care with the same foster parents for 18 months or more so that separation from them would adversely affect the child's development.

[NOTE: Unlike the handicapped definition, the definition of hard to place is inclusive, meaning a child must fit one of these specific categories to qualify as hard-to-place.]

North Carolina

State Subsidy Contact Person

Amelia Lance
DHR/DSS-Adoptions
2409 Mail Service Center
Raleigh, NC 27699-2409
Phone: 919-733-9464 x260
Fax: 919-733-3052
E-Mail: Amelia.Lance@ncmail.net

North Carolina's legal definition of special needs is as follows:

There exists, with respect to the child, a specific factor or condition (such as ethnic background, age, membership in a minority or sibling group, or the presence of factors such as medical conditions or physical, mental, or emotional handicaps) because of which it is reasonable to conclude that such child cannot be placed with adoptive parents without providing adoption assistance or medical assistance. These factors include:

Handicap—Known and diagnosed medical, mental, or emotional conditions that will require periodic treatment or therapy of a medical or remedial nature. Children who are known or suspected to be victims of sexual abuse would be considered to be in this category.

Potential Handicap—Hereditary tendency, congenital problem, birth injury, or other documented high risk factor leading to substantial risk of future disability. Such high risk factors may include, but are not limited to, the following: birth parents' mental illness and/or substance abuse of birth parents, separation trauma due to child's age at removal from birth parents' care, number of substitute placements, etc.

Sibling Status—Member of a family group to be placed together.

Need for Placement with Known and Approved Family—Such family would find the child's care an undue financial burden without Adoption Assistance. This includes relatives, other than biological parents, with whom a child has a close attachment, foster parents with whom a child has established a positive psychological bond and emotional tie, or other approved adoptive applicants deemed well suited to meet all but the financial component of the child's needs.

North Dakota

State Subsidy Contact Person

Julie Hoffman
Department of Human Services
Children and Family Services
600 East Boulevard Avenue
Bismarck, ND 58505
Phone: 701-328-4805; Fax: 701-328-3538
E-mail: sohofj@state.nd.us
Website: www.state.nd.us/humanservices/services/childfamily/adoption

North Dakota's legal definition of special needs is as follows:

A special needs child has at least one of the following characteristics:

a.   7 years of age or older;

b.   0-18 years with a physical, emotional, or mental disability or has been diagnosed by a licensed physician to be at high risk for such a disability;

c.   a member of a minority race; or

d.   member of a sibling group.

Ohio

State Subsidy Contact Person

Barbara Harris-Starks
Department of Jobs/Family Service
255 E. Main Street
Columbus, OH 43215
Phone: 614-466-9274
Fax: 614-728-2604
E-mail: harrib@odjfs.state.oh.us

Ohio's legal definition of special needs is as follows:

Federal IV-E Children: In order for a child to be considered a special needs child for the purposes of the adoption assistance program, all of the following criteria must be met:

A. The public children services agency (PCSA) has determined that the child cannot or should not be returned to the home of his parents.

B. The PCSA determined the child has a specific factor or condition(s) which indicates that in order to complete or sustain the adoption or ensure that the child's special needs are met, it is not in the child's best interest to be placed with adoptive parents without the provision of adoption assistance (AA) or medical assistance. A specific factor or condition shall include one or more of the following:

(1) membership in an ethnic or minority group; (2) age; (3) membership in a sibling group; (4) the presence of factors such as medical conditions or physical, mental, developmental or emotional disabilities; (5) emotional dependency upon foster parents; (6) factors in the child's medical history or background or the medical history background of the child's biological family place the child at risk to acquire a medical condition, a physical, mental or developmental disability or an emotional disorder; or (7) a disruption of an adoptive placement prior to the final decree of adoption which makes the child difficult to place with another adoptive family; or remaining in the permanent custody of a PCSA or PCPA for more than one year without being placed for adoption in spite of a plan of adoption for the child and reason-

able efforts documented by the PCSA or PCPA to place the child for adoption.

C. Unless the PCSA determines that it is against the best interest of the child to place the child with an adoptive family without the provision for AA or medical assistance, the PCSA or PCPA must document that a reasonable but unsuccessful effort was made to place the child with appropriate adoptive parents without providing AA. In making the determination that it is against the best interests of the child to be placed with an adoptive family without AA or medical assistance, the PCSA may site factors such as the existence of significant emotional ties to prospective adoptive parents which developed while in their care as a foster child or other factors pertaining to the child's current or anticipated special need for care or services.

State Non-IV-E Children: "Special Needs Child" is a child who has at least one of the following needs or circumstances that are barriers to his/her adoption, and adoption placement without financial assistance is unlikely because the child: (1) is in a sibling group who should be placed together; (2) is a member of a minority or ethnic group; (3) is 6 years of age or older; (4) has remained in the permanent custody of a PCSA or PCPA for more than one year; (5) has a medical condition, physical impairment, mental retardation or developmental disability; (6) has an emotional disturbance or behavior problem; (7) has a social or medical history or background or the child's biological family has a social or medical history which may place the child at risk of acquiring a medical condition, a physical, mental or developmental disability or an emotional disorder; (8) has been in the home of his/her prospective adoptive parents as a foster child for at least one year and would experience severe separation and loss if placed in another setting due to his/her significant emotional ties with these foster parents as determined and documented by a qualified professional psychologist; or (9) has experienced previous adoption disruption or multiple placements.

Oklahoma

State Subsidy Contact Person

Margaret DeVault
Department of Human Services (DHS)
P.O. Box 25352
Oklahoma City, OK 73125

Phone: 405-522-2467
Fax: 405-522-2433
E-mail: margaret.devault@okdhs.org

Oklahoma's legal definition of special needs is as follows:

A child must meet at least one or more of the following special needs criteria:

a.   Physical disability—a condition which requires regular treatment with a specific diagnosis given by the child's physician;

b.   Mental disability—the child must meet the eligibility criteria for educable multi-handicapped (EMH) or trainable multi-handicapped (TMH) classes and has been evaluated by a licensed psychologist, psychometrist, school, or recognized diagnostic center. A child with a demonstrable need for intensive adult supervision beyond ordinary age needs also qualifies;

c.   Age—if no other special needs criteria are met, child must be eight years of age or older. There is no age requirement for a child placed with a relative(s) who provides paid or non-paid kinship care and who meets the specified degree of relationship as defined in OAC 340:10-9-1;

d.   Sibling relationship—two siblings of any age may qualify without any additional conditions;

e.   Emotional disturbance—It is recognized that all children placed for adoption experience emotional disturbance. To meet this criteria, emotional disturbance must be (i) established by a physician, psychologist, behavioral therapist, or social worker; (ii) corroborated by a Child Welfare worker's observations of the child's behavior; (iii) corroborated by one or more caregiver such as a foster parent, Head Start or school personnel, church nursery, or child care provider; and (iv) documented with a specific diagnosis and prognosis, if applicable.

f.   Racial or ethnic factor—Indian, Hispanic, Oriental, and African-American children age three years or older;

g.   High risk of physical or mental disease—The child who exhibits high risk of physical or mental disease for conditions which are not presently being treated may qualify. If no other special factors or conditions are met, no monthly payment is made until there are documented symptoms of physical or mental disease. Indicators are: (i) social and medical histories of biological parents and family; (ii) events or life experiences such as severe sexual abuse; and (iii) prenatal exposure to drugs and alcohol.

Oregon

State Subsidy Contact Person

Kathy Ledesma
Adoption Assistance E71
Dept. of Human Services
Child, Adults and Families
Office of Permanency for Children
500 Summer Street NE
Salem, OR 97301-1068
Phone: 503-945-5677; Fax: 503-945-6969
E-mail: Kathy.Ledesma@state.or.us

or

Mary Ickes
(same address as above)
Phone: 503-945-5998; Fax: 503-945-6969
E-mail: Mary.Ickes@state.or.us

Oregon's legal definition of special needs is as follows:

The child has at least one of the following factors or conditions which make adoptive placement difficult to achieve: (a) has a documented medical, physical, emotional condition or other clinically diagnosed disability or has a documented history of abuse or neglect or other identified predisposing factor that places the child at risk for future problems and need for treatment; (b) is a member of a sibling group which will be placed together and is difficult to place because there are three or more children, or if in a sibling group of two, at least one of the children is six years of age or older; (c) is a member of an ethnic/racial/cultural minority (i.e. African American, Hispanic, Asian, Indian, Pacific Islander); (d) is eight years of age or older; or (e) has developed significant emotional ties with the prospective adoptive parents while in their care as a foster child (or relative placement), and the family needs financial and/or medical assistance in order to rear the child.

Pennsylvania

State Subsidy Contact Person

Cathy Utz
Department of Public Welfare
Office of Children, Youth & Families
P. O. Box 2675
Harrisburg, PA 17105
Phone: 717-705-2912
Fax: 717-705-0364
E-Mail: cutz@state.pa.us

Pennsylvania's legal definition of special needs is as follows:

The child shall have at least one of the following characteristics: (a) physical, mental, or emotional condition or handicap; (b) genetic condition which indicates a high risk of developing a disease or handicap; (c) member of a minority group; (d) member of a sibling group; (e) 5 years of age or older.

Rhode Island

State Subsidy Contact Person

Paula Fontaine
DCYF
560 Wood Street
Bristol, RI 02809
Phone: 401-254-7020
Fax: 401-254-7068
E-mail: Paula.Fontaine@dcyf.ri.gov

Rhode Island's legal definition of special needs is as follows:

A determination must be made that it is not in the child's best interest to return home.

B. A specific factor or condition, which could make the child difficult to place in an adoptive family without adoption assistance, must be present. The presence of one or more of these characteristics qualifies the child as "special needs." Such factors include:

a. has a documented mental condition or a physical, emotional, or mental disability;

b. is a member of an ethnic or racial minority;

c. is over the age of twelve;

d. is a member of a sibling group being adopted into the same home as a sibling;

e. has experienced a prior adoption disruption or dissolution; or

f. the child is at risk of developing a medical condition or a physical, emotional, or mental disability, based upon family background or history. In this situation, a child may be eligible for a deferred subsidy that would include a medical subsidy without financial assistance. In the event a disability (based upon family background or history) is diagnosed in the future, the child may then be eligible to receive financial assistance.

C. Reasonable efforts to place the child without adoption assistance must first be made, except in certain situations when a determination has been made by the Department that it is contrary to the child's best interests to be moved (e.g., a child being adopted by a relative who would not afford to adopt the child without subsidy).

South Carolina

State Subsidy Contact Person

Cathy Fitz
Department of Social Services
Division of Human Services, Adoption

P.O. Box 1520
Columbia, SC 29202
Phone: 803-898-7561/ 800-922-2504
Fax: 803-898-7641
E-mail: cfitz@dss.state.sc.us

South Carolina's legal definition of special needs is as follows:

A legally free child for whom reasonable but unsuccessful efforts have been made to place without subsidy except where it would be against the best interest of the child because of significant emotional ties with foster parents and the child meets one or more of the following criteria:

1. a white child ten years old or older;

2. a black or mixed-race child six years or older;

3. a physically, mentally, or emotionally handicapped child or a child at risk for physical, mental, or emotional handicaps;

4. a member of a white sibling group of three or more children placed together, one of whom is at least six years of age, or a sibling group of four or more white children of any age placed together;

5. a member of a black or mixed-race sibling group of two or more children placed together, one of whom is at least six years of age, or a sibling group of three or more black or mixed-race children of any age placed together; or

6. a member of a sibling group of two or more children placed together, one of whom is a special needs child.

South Dakota

State Subsidy Contact Person

Patricia Reiss
Department of Social Services (DSS)
Kneip Building, 700 Governors Drive
Pierre, SD 57501
Phone: 605-773-3227

Fax: 605-773-6834
E-mail: Patricia.Reiss@state.sd.us

South Dakota's legal definition of special needs is as follows:

Special needs and circumstances include: (a) a child's age, race, or religion; (b) a child with a physical, emotional, neurological, or intellectual handicap or problem; (c) a sibling group that needs to be placed together; (d) a child needing a prosthesis, extensive ongoing or anticipated medical care, or therapy for speech, physical, or psychological problems; and (e) when adoption by the foster parents with whom the child is living is the only appropriate plan.

Tennessee

State Subsidy Contact Person

Vicki Patrick
Department of Children's Services/ Adoption Services
Cordell Hull Building, 8th Floor
436 Sixth Avenue North
Nashville, TN 37243-1290
Phone: 615-532-5637; Fax: 615-532-6495
E-mail: Vicki.Patrick@state.tn.us

Tennessee's legal definition of special needs is as follows:

One or more of the following characterize the child: (a) Caucasian child age nine and above; (b) any child with minority heritage, age five and above; (c) any child who has a severe physical or psychological handicap as diagnosed by a licensed physician, psychologist, or licensed clinical social worker; (d) sibling groups of three or more who are placed together for the purpose of adoption at the same time; (e) any child who is HIV positive; (f) any child whose life experiences include neglect (which rises to the level of severe child abuse as defined in T.C.A. 37-1-102 (b) (21)), physical abuse and/or sexual abuse.

Texas

State Subsidy Contact Person

Susan Klickman
Dept. of Family and Protective Services (DFPS)
Box 149030, Code E-557
Austin, TX 78714-9030
Phone: 512-438-3302; Fax: 512-438-3782
E-mail: susan.klickman@dfps.state.tx.us

Texas's legal definition of special needs is as follows:

a. The child must be less than 18 years old and meet one of the following criteria when the adoptive placement agreement is signed:

1. the child is at least six years old;

2. the child is at least two years old and a member of a minority group that traditionally creates a barrier to adoption;

3. the child is being adopted with a sibling or to join a sibling; or

4. the child has a verifiable physical, mental, or emotional handicapping condition, as established by an appropriately qualified professional through a diagnosis that address:

5. what the condition is; and

6. that the condition is handicapping.

b. The State must determine that the child cannot or should not be returned to the home of his parents.

c. A reasonable effort must be made to find an adoptive placement without providing adoption assistance, unless doing so is against the child's best interests.

Utah

State Subsidy Contact Person

Ms. Marty Shannon
Department of Human Services
Division of Child and Family Services

120 North 200 West, #225
Salt Lake City, UT 84103
Phone: 801-538-3913
Fax: 801-538-3993
E-mail: mshannon@utah.gov

Utah's legal definition of special needs is as follows:

A child with special needs meets one of the following conditions: (a) the child is five years of age or older; (b) the child is under the age of 18 with a physical, emotional, or mental handicap; or (c) the child is a member of a sibling group placed together for adoption.

Vermont

State Subsidy Contact Person

Diane Dexter
Social Services Division
103 South Main Street
Waterbury, VT 05671-6531
Phone: 802-241-2142; Fax: 802-241-2407
E-mail: ddexter@srs.state.vt.us

Vermont's legal definition of special needs is as follows:

There exists with respect to the child a specific factor or condition which makes it reasonable to conclude that the child cannot be placed with adoptive parents without providing assistance. Such conditions include: race or ethnic background, age, membership in a sibling group, or the presence of factors such as medical conditions or physical, mental, or emotional handicaps.

Virginia

State Subsidy Contact Person

Brenda Kerr
Department of Social Services (DSS)

730 East Broad Street
Richmond, VA 23219
Phone: 804-692-1273
Fax: 804-692-1284
E-mail: bjk2@dss.state.va.us

Virginia's legal definition of special needs is as follows:

Children possessing one or more of the following factors: (a) physical, mental, or emotional condition existing prior to adoption; (b) hereditary tendency, congenital problem or birth injury leading to substantial risk of future disability; (c) age of six years or older; (d) minority or mixed racial heritage; (e) membership in a sibling group that should not be separated; (f) development of a meaningful relationship with foster parents with whom the child has resided.

[Note: This last criteria is applicable to state-funded subsidy only. The residency in question must have been for 12 months or longer.]

Washington

State Subsidy Contact Person

Lonni Locke
DSHS/Division of Program & Policy
Children's Administration
Adoption Support
P.O. Box 45713/MS-5713
Olympia, WA 98504
Phone: 360-902-7932/800-562-5682
Fax: 360-902-7903
E-mail: lolo300@dshs.wa.gov
LaShonda Proby, ICAMA Administrator
Phone: 360-902-7959
E-mail: pro1300@dshs.wa.gov

Washington's legal definition of special needs is as follows:

"Special needs" means the specific factors or conditions that apply to the child and that may prevent the child from being adopted unless the department provides adoption support services.

To be considered a child with special needs the following three statements must be true:

1. One or more of the following factors or conditions must exist:

    a. The child is of a minority ethnic background;

    b. The child is six years of age or older at the time of application for adoption support;

    c. The child is a member of a sibling group of three or more or of a sibling group in which one or more siblings meets the definition of special needs;

    d. The child is diagnosed with a physical, mental, developmental, cognitive or emotional disability; or

    e. The child is at risk for a diagnosis of a physical, mental, developmental, cognitive or emotional disability due to prenatal exposure to toxins, a history of serious abuse or neglect, or genetic history.

2. The state has determined that the child cannot or should not be returned to the home of the biological parent; and

3. The department or child placing agency that placed the child for adoption must document that, except where it would be against the best interests of the child, the department or child placing agency had made a reasonable but unsuccessful effort to place the child for adoption without adoption support.

West Virginia

State Subsidy Contact Person

Carolyn Phillips
Dept. of Health & Human Resources (DHHR)
Children and Adult Services
350 Capitol Street, Room 691
Charleston, WV 25301-3704

Phone: 304-558-7980
Fax: 304-558-4563
E-mail: carolynphillips@wvdhhr.org

West Virginia's legal definition of special needs is as follows:

West Virginia Code § 49-2-17 on subsidized adoption: "Children who are dependents of the department, or a child welfare agency licensed to place children for adoption, legally free for adoption and in special circumstances either because they(a) have established emotional ties with prospective adoptive parents while in their care, or(b) are not likely to be adopted by reason of one or more of the following conditions:

1. physical or emotional disability;

2. emotionally disturbed;

3. older children;

4. part of a sibling group;

5. member of a racial or ethnic minority; or

6. any combination of these conditions.

DHHR adoption policy further expands the definition of special needs to include children who appear healthy and of normal development but whose prognosis is guarded due to incest, mental illness or retardation of parent, drug use by parent, venereal disease of parent, or children with other impediments to adoption, such as long-term alternative care, or social or genetic complications in their family background.

Wisconsin

State Subsidy Contact Person

Jill Duerst
Department of Health & Social Services
PO Box 8916, 1 Wilson Street
Madison, WI 53708-8916

Phone: 608-266-1142
Fax: 608-264-6750
E-mail: duersjm@dhfs.state.wi.us
Web: http://dhfs.wisconsin.gov/children/adoption

Wisconsin's legal definition of special needs is as follows:

The child shall have at least one of the following special needs at the time of the adoptive placement: (a) 10 years of age or older (if age is the only factor in determining eligibility); (b) member of a sibling group of three or more children that must be placed together; (c) exhibits special need characteristics judged to be moderate or intensive under difficulty-of-care schedules; d) belongs to a minority race, and children of that race cannot be readily placed due to a lack of appropriate placement resources; or (e) a child at risk of developing a moderate or intensive level of special needs

(See http://www.legis.state.wi.us/rsb/code/hfs/hfs050.pdf)

Wyoming

State Subsidy Contact Person

Maureen Clifton
Department of Family Services (DFS)
130 Hobbs Avenue
Cheyenne, WY 82009
Phone: 307-777-3570; Fax: 307-777-3693
E-mail: mclift@state.wy.us

Wyoming's legal definition of special needs is as follows:

Special needs children are those who exhibit any or all of the following characteristics: (a) irreversible or non-correctable physical or mental disabilities; (b) physical, mental, or emotional disabilities correctable through surgery, treatment, or other specialized services; (c) six years of age or older; (d) been in the same foster family home for a lengthy period of time and emotional ties have developed; (d) racial minority; and/or (e) member of a sibling group needing to be placed in the same home as the siblings.

State-by-State definition of special needs child for subsidy is provided by National American Council on Adoptable Children, (NACAC).

APPENDIX D

Helpful Websites

Adoption—Friendly Workplace www.adoptionfriendlyworkplace.org
Employers can offer adoption benefits

Adoption Law Site www.adoptionlaw.org
General information regarding adoption law

Adoptive Families of America www.adoptivefam.org
Resource for families before, during and after adoption

Casey Family Program www.casey.org
Advocates for children in foster care

Child Welfare League of America (CWLA) www.cwla.org
Promotes foster care adoption, listing of state fact sheets

Children Rights www.childrensrights.org
Focuses on creating beneficial changes in child welfare systems

Dave Thomas Foundation for Adoption www.
davethomasfoundationforadoption.org
Dedicated to increasing the adoptions through the foster care system

Fostering Families Today www.fosteringfamiliestoday.com
Resource for foster care adoptions

Freddie Mac Foundation www.freddiemacfoundation.org
Adoptive and Foster parent resource

Internal Revenue Service www.irs.gov
Tax benefits information for adoptive and foster parents

National Adoption Center (NAC) www.adopt.org
National photolisting of waiting children

National Adoption Information Clearinghouse http://naic.acf.hhs.gov
Offers a wealth of adoption information for prospective adoptive parents, adoptive parents and adoptee

National Child Welfare Resource Center for Adoption (NCWRCA) www.nrcadoption.org
Special needs adoptions

National Foster Parent Association (NFPA) www.nfpainc.org
Supports foster parents
North American Council on Adoptable Children www.nacac.org
Conducts training for parent support groups and offers a wealth of information on adoption subsidies

Spaulding for Children www.spaulding.org
Promotes foster care adoption and provides training for professionals, organizations and parents

The Collaboration to AdoptUSKids www.adoptuskids.org
Photolisting of US waiting children

APPENDIX E

Suggested Reading

Best, Mary Hopkins. *Toddler Adoption: The Waevaer's Craft*. Indianapolis: Perspective Press, 1998

Hoppenhauer, Denise Harris. *Adopting a Toddler*. Lincoln, NE: iUniverse, 2002

Fahlberg, Vera, M.D. *A Child's Journey Through Placement*. Indianapolis: Perspective Press, 1991

Pertman, Adam. *Adoption Nation*. New York: Basic Books, 2000

Crain, Connie and Duffy, Janice. *How To Adopt a Child*. Tennesse: Thomas Nelson, Inc., 1994

O'Malley, Beth. *LifeBooks*: Winthrop, Mass: Adoption-Works, 2004

Wolff, Jana. *Secrets Thoughts of an Adoptive Mother*. Kansas City, MO: Andrews and McMeel, 1997

Kingsbury, Karen. *A Treasury of Adoption Miracles*. New York, NY: Warner Faith, 2005

Lancaster, Kathy. *Keys To Parenting An Adopted Child*. Hauppauge, NY: Barron's Educational Series, Inc, 1996

Robinson Grace. *Older Child Adoption*. New York, NY: The Crossroad Publishing Company, 1998

978-0-595-37700-
0-595-37700-9

Printed in the United States
119873LV00002B/80/A

9 780595 377008